Wm. H. Owen

Yale '97

Feb. 1939

YOU CAN FIND GOD

YOU CAN FIND GOD

BY
EDWARD SHILLITO

WILLETT, CLARK & COMPANY
CHICAGO   NEW YORK
1937

107722

239 T
8h62

English Edition
by Rich & Cowan, Ltd.

CONTENTS

YOU CAN FIND GOD

INTRODUCTION

IT IS high time that those who speak of the Christian gospel drop the apologetic tone. Our Lord is either the mighty Redeemer, living in the power of an endless life, or he is simply a dead hero about whom the world in the present time will be little concerned. A Christ reduced to the stature of a noble man of ancient times will interest nobody. The battle will rage, and it will be a fierce battle, between those who deny him and those who glory in him. The others will be brushed aside.

For himself and his own part in such a book as this the writer can think of a thousand apologies. For the gospel of our Lord Jesus Christ he is not prepared to offer one single by-your-leave; it is still the power of God whereby alone mankind, church, each nation and the family of nations, can be delivered.

It is high time that Christian teachers ceased to offer the Word on the ground that it will be useful through aiding mankind to meet the perils of upheavals and revolutions in human society. It is not first of all to be commended as beneficial, but as true. Some defenders of the faith appear to argue that here in Christ is a valuable framework for human society. It is as when the squire used to go to church in order to set a good example and to preserve order in the parish!

Or as when a man is honest because it is the best
policy. The gospel is not a device for preserving
things as they are. It does bring healing for nations,
as well as for individual souls, but never for those who
seek to use it and not first of all yield to its demands.
When they would have made Jesus king, he withdrew
himself from the midst of them. That he will still do,
if we think that we shall use him.

It is high time that in our discussions of religion we
be not afraid of the name of God. We have yielded
too long to the defect of our religious thinking, that
we are much more willing to talk of synagogics — that
is, of things which concern the organization of the
church — than of God. As a character in Mr. Hum-
bert Wolfe's satire says:

> " When He ventures to intrude
>   He doesn't seem the Bible's voice of thunder
>   So much as a distressing social blunder."

The time for this cowardice, which is falsely called
reverence, is past; and it is a cause for thankfulness
that among the youth of today there is a growing readiness to demand from Christian teachers that they be
not apologetic upon the one theme which matters.
They ask of the church: " What have you to tell us
about God? That is your business! "

It is high time that we made once more our appeal to the individual soul. " Individualism is dead,"
many maintain. " There is no life which is not lived
in community. There is no such thing as a churchless
Christianity." All these things are true. But it does
not follow that there are not decisions of critical importance to be made in the individual mind and con-

science. It still is of importance if somewhere a Saul of Tarsus sees a light brighter than that of noon, or if a John Wesley has his heart strangely warmed. This book is written in the belief that the reader, without tarrying for any, can himself go out in search of God; and that once more the Lord says: " What is that to thee? Follow thou me."

It is high time that we listened once more to the words of St. Paul: " Wherefore he saith, Awake thou that sleepest and arise from the dead, and Christ shall give thee light."

It is high time that in the music of the Christian church we hear again in such words the sound of the silver trumpet. The days are over in which any other summons will be heard by the desperate children of men. But times are such that the brave will welcome the hazards and the terrors of the conflict. In the tumult Christ their Lord will draw near to them, and with him they will walk unafraid into the unknown future.

DO WE WANT TO FIND GOD?

WE CAN find God, but do we want to find him?

It cannot be said that all men are seeking for him, nor of any man that he is always seeking for him. At the most it can be claimed that every man at some time in this life has believed in a God who is found by those who seek him, and few men have not set out upon that search, even if they have taken only a few steps.

It is well not to take too much for granted. We have to deal with man as he is, and not set up an imaginary being, either too spiritual on the one hand or too animal on the other. We must begin where we are. "If it is to Dublin you are going," the Irishman said to the inquirer, "I wouldn't start from here." If it is our purpose to look for God, we may find it hard to start from here. We might wish for some other starting point; but there is none. The first of all conditions in this as in all journeys is that, being what we are, we should deal with things as they are and set out from where we are.

Nothing is more fatal than to play tricks with the factors which make up a problem. The schoolboy who juggles the working of a sum in order to reach the answer which he has looked up, is simply wasting his time. He will either remain in ignorance, or have to return to the very beginnings of his subject. We, too, if we would enter upon the search for God, must not cook up the answer. This we do if we set up for ourselves an imaginary being who has no relation to the real man, and follow his search.

For it is we who must seek. We — not the seekers of other days with the facts as they dealt with them; not those spiritual athletes whose records we can study in biographies; not the mystics, who must have God; not Enoch, who walked with him, nor Moses, who spoke with him as a man speaks to his friend. Our case is not theirs; and the question is whether we, not such as they, can find God. We, as we are today, not as we were in other years; not as we might have been today if we had lived differently. We, with our past written and never to be unwritten. We, with our master interests already determined, with grooves in our thinking, now both deep and wide; with our characters shaped so that our friends make allowance for us and say harshly or tolerantly, "We must not forget that he is timid, or selfish, or quick-tempered, or self-indulgent." Do we, being such as we are, want to find God?

When Jesus called Simon to follow him, he did not call a man about whom nothing distinctive could be said. It was not man, but this man whom he called. He saw in Simon an individual unit, waiting for that call. In Simon lived the memory of his race. He was what he was because patriarchs had fought with the angel of God for God's blessing, and seers had passed into the thick darkness where God was; a thousand lives lived on in him. Simon was not one of a crowd, indistinguishable from the rest. He was

now to make a new beginning, but he did not cast
off his character and disposition. He was that Simon
who had been an impulsive boy, and a man rash and
easily moved, and he would still be the same. So we
see him at Caesarea Philippi saying at one moment,
"Thou art the Christ," and at the next, when his
Master spoke of the cross, becoming the spokesman
of the Tempter, "Be this far from thee." Simon was
himself as he had been and he was now also a distinctive being who held the key to many lives. Between the past ages and the hidden future there was
this being. Jesus sought him. He had to start from
where he was, being the man that he was. So he left
his nets and followed him.

The mystic will not be interested in a book with the
title, *You Can Find God.* Of course he can find
God. But the spiritual man, mystic or not, does not
claim any special table for himself. He does not set
himself above the others. He does not claim a place
at the right hand of the King. Why should he? He
knows that in the sight of the eternal Lord men are
not far removed from one another. From that height
the low foothills and the snow-clad mountaintops are
not so distant from each other as they look to us. The
spiritual man does not give himself airs. He seeks no
private entrance to the temple. What he has found
anyone may find. What has he that he did not first
receive?

But it is not with such a man, disciplined already
by long years of hardship on pilgrimage, that this book
has to do. He may think of himself as on our level,
but we cannot think of ourselves as on his. Nor can
we take shelter behind him and play at being like him,

using his words and borrowing his visions. We must not live on borrowed capital. "Ye hypocrites, ye actors," Jesus said, and he spoke not to Pharisees alone. We may miss God through pretending that we have found him.

It is with us, as we are in our present condition, that this book has to do.

The Christian faith is not meant for the mystic and the spiritual only. There is not, and there can never be, an inner area reserved for the few, while the many must be left to content themselves with an outer realm. It is perhaps a pity that when we meet a Christian we *will* call him a mystic. No church is worthy of the name which has nothing to give to the unspiritual. The Lord of the church was known as the friend of publicans and sinners, and the church is not above its Lord. Men have left certain churches because they found everything in their worship and their community life arranged on the supposition that everyone who took part was spiritual. Their language was in the key of an unearthly devotion. Hymns told of aspirations which only the saints in their hours of vision could feel. The language, long after the revival is over, is kept in the key set in seasons of revival. How could those who do not share such raptures be anything but interlopers, like strangers who find themselves by some error in a select house party? The church is no church which provides only for a house party of saints.

It is no defense of such a church to appeal to the New Testament; unreal language is often used of the early churches which are described in its pages. But however high their standards it is plain that they made provision for the unspiritual man who had yet to make the first steps in the Way, and they were long-suffering with him. In what church, except in the mission field, could we meet today saints as imperfect, and indeed as unspiritual, as some of those with whom St. Paul worshiped in Corinth? The early church was a school for saints, but a school with many departments and with provision for backward scholars.

But however strange and embarrassing a spectacle the plain man may think himself to be in some churches, he need have no fear that he is strange or unwanted in the presence of the Lord of the church. Christ's word is still, " Him that cometh unto me, I will in no wise cast out "; this is the open invitation which is in the very character of the gospel. It is not to the spiritual genius, but to every man, that the good news is brought, and the Lord Christ still hides many things from the wise and prudent and reveals them to babes. There are strange warnings that those are last here which shall be first.

We need not pretend to be other than we are. We may even discover as we proceed on the journey that the spiritual man is not one who is enriched by a sixth sense, but that he is very much like ourselves in his gifts. He is not in a class by himself. What he has become we may become. In any case, without waiting for exalted moods and without hiding our real character, we can begin the search for the living God.

It is not a God undefined for whom we have to seek, but *this* God; it is not anyone in general who is called to the search, but you.

Where we are: that is our starting point. Simon and Andrew started from their fishing nets, Levi from his customs table. It may be said that they left their old ways not because they were seeking, but because they had found their Lord. "We have found him of whom Moses and the prophets spoke," they said. But their obedience to the call was also the beginning of a life of adventure in which they were hammered and forged into instruments for the divine purpose. They, being such as they were, rose up and followed their Lord. The one condition they were ready to meet: They *did* want to seek; they *did* desire above all things to find God. They were at the beginning of a new life, pilgrims and seekers always.

Do we want to find God? From among those who make no claims to "being religious," as they put it, and are frankly unspiritual, there are many answers to this question.

One man says: "I have never given it much thought. I leave such matters to others. If I go to church, I go in the hope that I may find some help in doing my duty and in living a better life, but I do not think of seeking for God — that is above me; such words only suggest memories of the Scriptures or the language of hymns or sermons. I cannot honestly use them."

Another answers: "On the contrary, I do my best now to escape from all such thoughts. I remember a long time ago hearing preachers who stirred me for a short time; but that passed, and I have no desire to be moved again as I was then. Moody nearly had me once. But I got away and thought twice over the matter. Besides, it is on the cards that there may be nothing in religion at all. We shall die, and we may never know that we are dead." How much of such talk is bravado we cannot say; but no one need go far to hear it.

Still another man says that his hour of interest in religion came with the uprising of love within him in the days of youth.

> " Love wakes men once a lifetime each;
>   They lift their heavy lids and look,
>   And, lo, what one sweet page can teach,
>   They read with joy, then shut the book." *

Love, he will explain, cast a glorious image on the screen of the universe; and this he took to be God.

Another has become entirely absorbed by the practical interests of his life. Slowly his outlook has been changed. His morning paper is always opened to the financial news first of all. Markets, amusements, sport — these are his real interests. He does not give himself much time to think of religion. It sounds too much like something in the air. One world at a time, and this world, after all, is not a bad place. If there should prove to be a spiritual world he will come to know it in good time, and the God who rules it will not be too hard upon him; God will forgive — " that is his business."

Another makes a working arrangement: so long as he can keep the thought of God confined to the inner area of the individual life, he will gladly acknowledge him. But he must be allowed to say for himself what manner of God he is prepared to accept. He must be left free, for example, to say to any prophet, or apostle, or minister of the church that he cannot accept his

* Coventry Patmore.

teaching if he preaches a God who takes sides in practical matters of the business or social order. Religion, yes; but religion which accepts the present order of things; religion within the framework of things as they are.

But we cannot so " halve the gospel of God's grace "; we cannot make terms with God. The present order may be well suited to our tastes; but what right have we to assume that the Lord of the world makes special provision for us? Why should an order be preserved because it suits us? We cannot so limit God. If we want to find a God whose ways are designed to suit our needs, we shall look in vain.

Such answers reveal clearly how mistaken it is to suppose that men are either seeking for God or are miserable without him. No one verdict can be given. On the one side we have the words of St. Augustine that man is never at rest till he finds rest in God; on the other, the evidence everywhere that it is possible to pass through years of life without troubling about God at all. On the one hand there are those who find the peace which the world cannot give; on the other, those who find the peace which the world can and does give.

There are two kinds of conversion. There have been some, indeed, who have been converted not to God, but from him. One such man expressed regret in his old age that he had spent so many years without knowing the delights of a godless life. Can such a verdict be possible? We must remember that in this present life we have not enough evidence to make a verdict on life certain and unanswerable. We must not credit a man with the right to pronounce finally upon his own policy. It may prove true — we believe that it will — that the man who has lived godless without any distress of mind has missed the purpose of this life: he will know this afterward, but for the present he does not know.

Finding God, or trying to find him, is not a matter of what is called happiness. In the story of his life the Danish poet Jørgensen tells of a conversation between a freethinker and a French Catholic, a well known Parisian advocate.

" You are fortunate in being a believer," the freethinker said.

" You are quite mistaken, sir. One is not at all fortunate when one is a believer. It is the greatest misfortune that can happen to you, to become a Christian. . . . You are fortunate, who do not believe in anything! You order your life as you please and at the same time keep your good conscience, and very possibly you will get into heaven at last, as it is presumably through no fault of yours that you are a freethinker and a heathen. We others have received the gift of faith and the responsibility it entails, and it often weighs so heavily upon us that we nearly faint under it, as under the burden of a cross." *

A paradox is presented here which a French thinker would love. It is not the whole truth; but if by " fortunate " we mean what the ordinary man means by that word, it is true that the man without faith

* Johannes Jørgensen, *Autobiography*. English translation (Sheed & Ward), II, 217.

is often more fortunate than are those who enter the
kingdom of heaven. Much harm is done by those who
always speak as if the unbelievers or skeptics were
miserable. They used to delight in making legends
to prove it. It is certainly not true to the facts of
human society that mankind may be divided into the
fortunate who believe and the miserable who do not
believe. It is enough to say that no man must estimate
the value of his life until all the evidence is before him.
He may be happy enough now, but is that enough to
know? In one of his sudden flashes of insight St.
Augustine, telling of his early life, cried out, " But
was it life, O my God? "

How are we to account for the atheist? By that
term is meant not the serious thinker who has con-
vinced himself that there is no God, but the man who
has based his practical life on the thesis: " There is no
God." The atheist practices the absence of God. If
he seeks anything at all it is to escape from the last
traces of faith in God. He is not by any means unfamiliar in our society. The atheist of the school of
Ingersoll or Bradlaugh seldom raises his voice in these
days; the atheist who is in flight from God is a common figure.

The very name, " God," has linked to it certain
vague thoughts. It does not suggest anything which
the atheist would care to know better. It speaks of
a discipline which he resents. If he were to find the
God of whom he thinks hazily, he might be called to
make changes and even revolutions in his way of living.
So he becomes a pilgrim — a pilgrim hurrying away
from God.

Or he may be simply lazy or lacking in enterprise.

He goes the way of least resistance. That is not hard to understand. Most men are tempted to settle down in life. A few climb the heights, but most are happy enough to look at them on the screen or on the map. We are proud that we belong to the race which produced Columbus. But the world waited a long time for him. There was one Columbus, and the others were content to leave the voyaging to him.

" What if wise men had, as far back as Ptolemy,
 Judged that the earth like an orange was round?
 None of them ever said, Come along, follow me,
 Sail to the west and the east will be found."

It was not by processes of contemplation that America was discovered. The thinking had to be proved in action. There is always the temptation in religion to take the easy ways and to use the heroic speech without paying the price.

We may refuse to seek because we are not disposed to run the hazards or pay the price. The search for God is not to be undertaken as though it were a matter of book learning or speculation. A survey of the facts with which we have to do does not justify any simplification.

It is important in answering the question, " What is man really like? " and therefore, " What am I? " to remember the twofold character of human life. We have no right to forget that St. Francis and David Livingstone were men, and in a human life won their place among those of whom the world was not worthy, and of whom it is said that God is not ashamed to be called their God. On the other hand, there is the great multitude of those, also in our human company, who do not aspire to or set out upon any such adventures. We may be among them. We must not forget that we have fallen below our full stature. We may rise with Christ, but we may also escape from him. We are of the same family as St. Paul and Nero, as St. Francis and Borgia.

Thinking soberly is a first condition of our search. Soberly does not mean despairingly. This book would not be written if there were not in the very heart of man a capacity for this search. The question whether or not we can find God would not have been asked.

There are first of all two judgments to be rejected. Man is not to be treated either as a being who can hold his own before God with head lifted high and face unashamed, or as a being who is without any way by which God can approach him, without any language in which God can speak to him. Man can be neither presumptuous nor despairing. In him littleness and greatness meet. He is not to be considered either a seeker always after God or one who cannot seek for him at all. It is wiser to keep to the bold paradoxes of Holy Scripture and say at once that man is little and great, a sinful creature who may become one of the sons of God; he is lost, and yet may be found.

It may be against despair that we have to fight most resolutely. We may doubt human capacity for this endeavor. We may doubt man.

There is a legend of Moses told in Hebrew lore. Moses had asked of the Lord of the World why he could not cross the border and enter into the Promised Land.

Then God said: "Thou hast doubted me: I forgive thee. Thou hast doubted thyself: I forgive thee. But thou hast doubted Israel, thou hast doubted mankind, wherefore thou shalt not enter into this land of my promise. Israel is laden with defilements; but whence comest thou if it be not from Israel? . . . Men are cowardly, perverse, envious, lustful, lying, thieving, murderous and blaspheming: but what art thou, if not a man? What thou hast comprehended, me, wherefore should not the others one day comprehend it also? " *

Wherefore! Wherefore, if others like ourselves have journeyed and have seen and marveled, should not we also? True, we are conscious of all that makes it hard; but so were they. They attained; that is no reason for presumption, but it is a reason why we should not despair.

From within our mysterious nature come voices which vary in clearness and power. Some are only like echoes with a dying cadence. But there is one call to which we cannot always close our ears. Sometimes it brings to us a start of surprise, but something within us answers to it. "Before thou didst belong to this world of time, thou wert mine. I have graven thee upon mine hands, thou art mine."

If there were no such voice that we could hear and answer, how would the appeal of Book or Church, of Word or Sacrament come home to us? It is our confidence and our hope that we can hear. There is an inner land beneath the surface of life, like the con-

* Edmond Fleg, *Life of Moses*. English translation (Victor Gollancz), p. 213.

tinents below the sea . . . " the dark-grey level plains of ooze, where the shell-burr'd cables creep." It is because there is such a hidden life that the call to set out in search of God can be made with confidence. Whatever life may seem to be on the surface, it is not with that we have to do. However much, on the evidence of his outward life, man may despair of himself and of Israel, there is still the world within him with which he must reckon. He may keep the door of his life barred, but he will not escape from the sound of the knocking upon the door.

II

WHAT IS THIS LIFE GOOD FOR?

WE MAY or we may not seek for God, but we shall have to seek for something, or cease to be human.

When the call of God comes to men it is not the first call or the only call that reaches them. In this respect it is in keeping with their character. They are not homekeepers now for the first time called to leave their firesides, not knowing which way they are going. Religion is not against the grain of human life.

It is not open to anyone to say, " I am no seeker; why, then, should I seek God? " He may say, " I am seeking other things and I am not prepared to turn my energies to this search." He may not say, " I am going to stay at home; why, then, invite me to seek for God? " He can only say, " I have chosen some other road; I am not free to take this."

It may be argued that this human life has no purpose at all, that the race is one without a starting point and without a goal, without penalties and without rewards. There have always been those who are condemned to such skepticism, but man has always found it difficult to rest content with such a verdict. If it is an idiot's story, why does the idiot know this? When the idiot knows he is an idiot, is he any longer an idiot?

Or it may be that in the scene man is but an ac-

cidental variation of little meaning in the sum of
things. Of his own place in the universe man has
thought much; he has been troubled beyond measure
to know where he stands in the world of infinitely
great and infinitely little things. But some imagine
that he is only the victim of his own illusions. If that
is our belief, we must accept it and build our life on
this foundation. We must be content to write life
down neither as a tragedy nor as a divine comedy, but
as a modest tale of a creature who thought more highly
of himself than he should have thought, but discovered his error at last and settled down to a life
within strict limits and without aspiration.

But a place in which we lived without aspiration
would be much like hell. Indeed, this might be taken
as a definition of hell. " All hope abandon, ye who
enter here," were the words which Dante read at the
entrance to the Inferno. Any place is hell over which
such words could be written.

In the poem " Simpson's Choice," Clutton Brock
describes how Simpson wakes up in the life beyond
death to find, to his great delight, that his new scene
is exactly like the one in which he had lived a selfish
and worldly life. He had expected a worse fate. But
the devil explains to him that it is in reality hell to
which he has come. Of those who do not belong to
that realm the devil says:

" Death brings no peace to them, for they are cursed,
Just like fond mortals with immortal thirst
For beauty, love and knowledge and what not;
But here such vague abstractions are forgot.
No friend of mine has ever asked for wings;
We rest content with facts and concrete things."

But the place in which we live is not hell; it is earth, in which man still has longings and desires which will not let him rest. We are not doomed to despair or to settle down with things as they are. No such curse rests upon our race.

We may find strong evidence that man is not a blunder, that nature has not all unconsciously betrayed him, but that he is the heir of the world for whom all its history has been a preparation. In him, we believe, this world has come to its expression; the sealed orders under which all created things have moved have been broken. Is man the being for whom the whole creation groans and travails in pain — man as he is, called to be a son of God, heir of God and joint-heir with Christ?

It is not part of the task which this book attempts to fulfill to present a case for this view of man. It is accepted at the outset that he is not deceived in his aspirations. If this claim were to be dismissed, then the belief that man can find God would fall to the ground. Only on the condition that human life is no mistake and no scene of illusion can we consider the call to seek the Lord.

But if we believe that there is a purpose then we shall inquire what this purpose is, or, in other words, " What is the place good for? " There can scarcely be any doubt that if it is good for anything at all, it is as a place of struggle and conflict, whereby the creature man is educated for his calling. Or, if we take the words of our Lord, it is a place meant for those who ask, seek, knock; and the asking, seeking, knocking are not optional but essential. Not otherwise can man come to his place in the eternal world; not otherwise are the sons of God to be revealed. Creation waits for that apocalypse.

In our imagination we may see this as a world of a different character, one in which everything is provided for its inhabitants without conflict or difficulty on their part. They receive without asking, they find without seeking, and without their knocking doors open to them. They have no need to dig the earth or sail the seas to win their bread. They have no mysteries to explore, no enemies to meet, no tragedy to purify their hearts with terror. All is as neat and tidy as in some heaven of H. G. Wells. Such a world might have been, but it is not this world as we know it. The creatures that inhabited it would not be entitled to the name of human. Nor will it serve any useful purpose to inquire what the policy of our life might be in such a world. We have to do with a scene of another kind in which man, if he has any meaning at all, is a being disciplined and schooled by struggle for some hidden and amazing purpose.

If this is a drama with any plot at all it is a divine drama, and its title is, *The Coming of the Sons of God*; and God's sons can come into their glorious destiny only by taking their part in an action in which there is no sham fight. In this drama there are no earthly spectators. The children of earth, if they are to come to themselves, must be prepared in that drama not for peace but for the sword. They are not marionettes pulled by strings, soon, when their entertainment is over, to be put back in the box. They are real beings in a world which is no illusion. They must seek as living actors, and seeking is in the very character of the place they live in.

If any man abandons the scene of action and thinks that he has found in passivity the end of life, he is deceived. He has not found the true end; he is a deserter. That is why in the judgment books of earth a severer verdict is passed upon those who stand aside than upon those who make many blunders and commit many sins, but do take part in the conflict. The wrath of all true servants of God is reserved chiefly for those who are spectators. When, in one of the oldest of songs, we read how Deborah called the Israelites to battle, we see that her curse rested upon the men of Meroz " because they came not to the help of the Lord, to the help of the Lord against the mighty." They came not; they tarried at home; they won the reproach which always rests upon Meroz, the land where men rest when others are fighting.

Once more, man is a seeker; that is not a part which he can take up and lay down as he pleases and still be a man — it is a distinctive mark of his manhood; it is the very definition of his character.

What is man? In natural history man takes his place among the other creatures of this earth. He indeed shares much with those which we call subhuman. The apes of the forest have some things in common with human beings. They can be taught to imitate their ways. Those who have seen a chimpanzee smoke a cigar, or eat at table, will easily understand what is shared with man by the other creatures which inhabit this earth. Like man, they have their foes to fight; they have their own kind to defend. But the apes are not seekers in the sense in which man is a seeker. They hunt, it is true, for food; they move to fresh forests when the food fails. They are in the midst of foes; they must watch. But they have no desire to move into the mists which hang like a shroud over an unknown sea; they do not know the pressure upon them of the mysterious universe; they are not as man is in his noblest representatives — prepared to stake all that he has upon the search for truth. Other creatures are not hungry for knowledge.

It cannot be claimed, as we have seen, that all men have this hunger; or indeed that any man is always hungry after truth. But the quality is one which marks man, though it is neither universal nor perpetual. Where man is like the subhuman creatures he needs no special explanation; we can understand him there. It is where he differs that we begin to see what man is, and man only.

When the first adventurer set out in his cockleshell boat upon the seas, not knowing what was before him, no doubt the others mocked at him and in their comfortable caves congratulated themselves upon their security. " Poor fellow! " they said. " What a pity that he is not like other men! " They piled up their fires, and shut out the storm, and were proud that they were normal men. They even said that there was something abnormal about the seeker. Yet, looking back to the beginnings of humanity we know that the mad sailor was the one of that company who came nearest to being a man. The others could be easily explained as variations of an animal stock. The seeker calls for some other name.

To this day it is clear that of the children of men the majority are content to leave mysteries unexplored. What it is like on the roof of the world we are con-

tent to let others tell us. What may be the sources
of the great rivers we do not trouble to inquire. We
fit ourselves into the world of things as we have received it. Explorers, travelers, scholars are for us the
rare, unusual, odd men. We who are not putting ourselves out to seek a way into the unknown are the
ordinary, sensible, normal men. Yet at the same time
we cannot escape altogether from the suspicion that
actually they may be the normal and we the odd people. It may be human to seek, and less than human
to accept things as they are. We read the stories of
Scott and Shackleton and Edward Wilson; by all
standards of prudence these men were clearly mad or,
as our familiar phrase puts it, " beside themselves."
But something in us prompts us to believe that in
truth they are not beside themselves at all; they have
come to themselves. They have arrived; it is we who
have halted on the way. It is we others who are beside ourselves. Such, then, is man the seeker.

If we turn to the writings from which we learn
the way of life, we discover to our amazement that
man in this historic scene, when he has been most
clearly man, has always been searching not only after
knowledge, but also after God. He has sought since
the days when Enoch walked with God and " listened
continually to the Voice." The men of whom this
world was not worthy were not content to take things
as they were and to limit themselves to the visible
earth. They went out, not knowing whither they
went, but sure that there was a City with foundations,
and they must not rest till they found it. We catch
sight in Ur of the Chaldees of a sheik, the head of a
clan, rich in possessions. There was no reason but

one why he should leave Ur of the Chaldees, but that one reason outweighed all others — prudence, common sense, tradition, the love of peace. He was not driven by hunger or by any of the untamed forces of nature. There were many wandering caravans in that country, but his was not of that kind. He had heard a voice which he could not deny or disobey. He became a seeker because of that voice within him. The father of the men of faith in all ages went out not knowing whither he went, nor was Abraham strange and inhuman in so doing.

This is always the story of man when he enters upon his distinctive life. He is a pilgrim setting out upon the road at whose end is " the hope of the city of God."

Man has never ceased, and can never cease, from his search for the hidden secrets of his world. Edward Wilson put clearly the reason why this search must not cease, however great the price to be paid for it. Speaking of the Antarctic Expedition in which he took part, he said: " As for its main object, the acquisition of knowledge pure and simple, surely God means us to find out all we can of his works, and to work out our own salvation, realizing that all things that have to do with our spiritual development are understood and clearly seen." To read God's thoughts after him is the calling which comes to man; he disobeys it at his peril.

The leaders in this search must deny themselves: they are poor; their lives are cut short; their days are spent in toil which brings little reward in their time save the joys of obedience and adventure and, it may

be, of the vision which comes in some hour of achieve-
ment. But these are the men who forever set the
standard for others. It is written of another of the
explorers of our time, who died upon Mount Everest:
" Mallory was burning with a kind of fire, an ardent
spiritual soul, winding himself up to a passion of effort
the higher he got." Such ardent impatient souls miss
many treasures, but they win that for which this life
is most worth living.

But is this search for knowledge to be separated
from that desire to know God of which the records
of mankind are full? We can appeal, if we will, to
those records. We can call as witnesses seekers after
knowledge in every age. We shall never escape from
the evidence that in all their seekings they have known
themselves to be seeking for God. There are many
sacred places to which man may go on pilgrimage. The
earth is filled with witnesses to the past hopes and
dreams of mankind. But whenever men bring to light
the hidden dwelling places of their ancestors they find
sacred buildings in which man impressed upon stone
his aspirations after God. We never find man without
aspiration in history. Losing aspiration, he would have
ceased to be man. And these many aspirations are
not left scattered and unrelated; they are fulfilled in
one paramount desire. What man has won on each
level of life is carried over to the level on which, with
all his treasures of wisdom and knowledge, he seeks
the Lord.

Sometimes in certain ages it looks as if the old desire had died down; but suddenly, without warning,
it flames up again, and the fierce cry arises to God

from some quiet and sensitive soul: "I must have thee"; and the things which had grown old become new.

It is in such a world that our story must be written. This is the character of our race, where it has been graven deep in its annals. We belong to a race whose seekers have always been on the track of God.

We shall be wise to accept this fact. We have no other course. The familiar story of Carlyle is not without its bearing upon this matter. Someone explained to him one day that Margaret Fuller "accepted the universe." "Gad! she'd better!" Carlyle replied. We had better adjust ourselves to the world as it comes to us, and not dream idly of another world in which we might have followed another way of life. If we accept the character of human life as it is given to us for a scene of conflict and pilgrimage, we shall not seek for the peace which eternity may bring to us; we shall live now as the dwellers in this mansion — no peaceful mansion — of the Father's house, and try with all diligence to win the good gift which can be won here. We must enter with full knowledge of what is involved into the ranks of the seekers. "We accept our calling to seek the Lord, if haply we may feel after him and find him."

It is not always a question whether a thing in itself is good or evil. Often the decisions we must make are decisions between the good which is fitting to our present life and some other good.

No complete analogy can be found, but one of partial significance may be used. A certain man after saving for years was able to spend a holiday in a Swiss village. It was spring. The fields were decked with flowers. The snows were white " so as no fuller on earth can white them." Cataracts leaped down every hillside. The land lay smiling in the sunshine and frowning in the storm. But this man settled down in his hotel. He read books; he played chess; he put records on the phonograph — all excellent activities in themselves. But the days passed by, and he never saw the light of the morning on those hills, or the blue of the lake, or the embroidery of the flowers. He went home again, but he had not seen Switzerland. He had not found the thing for which that place was good.

One would think that no man could be so incredibly stupid as this. But in the concerns of this earthly life men constantly, blindly, are doing this very thing. They miss the distinctive character of this life. They may be busy about things not in the least evil, but they will go out of this life without the treasure which it was meant to give to them. They may win many gains, but not the one thing this earth could give to them.

It may be that God could have ordered our life for us so that we might have him without seeking. But certainly this he has not done, and we should not waste our time in dwelling upon such speculations. He might have ordained for us a settled life; he has called us to be pilgrims. He might have given us peace; he gives us war, and war to the end. Having done all, we are to stand ready for the next battle.

We have now to accept life as he gives it to us. We are pilgrims and we must now live as pilgrims. We are soldiers and we must not lay aside our arms.

" If this for me is thy command,
  To serve within a threaten'd land,
Where every day a conflict brings
  To outposts of the King of kings,

" Then, Lord of Hosts, my glory lies
  In restless watch of sleepless eyes,
In heart that leaps to join the fight
  At dawn or noon or black midnight."

" The night cometh when no man can work." Life is as one long day. This day must end, and when it ends it is not reborn. Another day may dawn, but in that day other work will be found for us. The work of the today must be done punctually. In the business of life there is no working overtime.

In eternity, it is sometimes said, there will be no battles to wage, no wrongs to right; the soldier will be delivered from his campaigning and the pilgrim will be home.

That may be. But what follows if this is so? If there is anything to be won in this day, surely it must be won now. If the adventure and the discipline, the sorrow and the joy of the pilgrim are to be ours, they must be ours now. The night cometh. . . .

III

ALONG WHAT ROADS?

I want you, just because you long for religion, to continue to cultivate, to cultivate more carefully and lovingly also, the interests, the activities, that are not directly religious. And this, not simply because, " Why, of course, we must eat our dinner; of course, we must have our little relaxations "; but much more because without these not directly religious interests and activities you — however slowly and unperceivedly — lose the material for grace to work in and on.*

IF IT is granted that man is a seeker, and so long as he does not seek he falls below his proper life; and if all his seekings are gathered up in one — the search for God — what roads are open to him? From the place where he is now, what ways branch out for him to take? There may be more than one.

We have always to guard ourselves against considering plans or journeys as alternatives when they are not. There is no need to say at the outset " either . . . or "; we may have both. It is true that we shall come to crossroads at which we shall be challenged to make a choice; but too often we are tempted to say, when there is no necessity, " I choose this and not that ";

* Baron von Hügel, *Letters to a Niece* (J. M. Dent and Sons, Ltd.), p. 62.

to take one or the other when we might have both.

We may begin with the truth that man's life has more levels than one. There is no reason at the outset to say that we can find God only on one level. We may look for him on each level, though not in the same way. Man has a physical life in which he must ask, seek and knock, or he will perish. He has an intellectual life in which he uses his physical powers in the quest of knowledge. Walter de la Mare writes in his poem, " Miss T.":

> " It's a very odd thing —
>   As odd as can be —
> That whatever Miss T. eats
>   Turns into Miss T.;
> Porridge and apples,
>   Mince, muffins and mutton,
> Jam, junket, jumbles —
>   Not a rap, not a button
> It matters; the moment
>   They're out of her plate,
> Though shared by Miss Butcher
>   And sour Mr. Bate;
> Tiny and cheerful
>   And neat as can be,
> Whatever Miss T. eats
>   Turns into Miss T." *

That is the life which Miss T. lives on one level, and the poem gives us the precise truth concerning it. We must not be ashamed in the least of this level. Whatever Shakespeare ate turned into Shakespeare the

* Walter de la Mare, *Peacock Pie* (Constable).

poet, who interpreted the way of life in all its windings and sounded all the deep places of the spirit of man. For him dinner was no humiliating concession but a delightful necessity.

No less is it true that whatever St. Francis ate turned into St. Francis. The necessary and often wearisome search for food and clothing is a condition without which other searches cannot begin. The physical level finds its meaning not in itself, but in other levels. By itself it is incomplete. The man who seeks for nothing but to carry on his physical life misses the meaning of even that life. He is what is called a splendid animal, and that means a splendid failure. The animal becomes splendid only when he uses his animal nature in the service of that which is more than animal.

Even in a perfectly ordered human life man would not be set free from all concern for his body. He would still keep in touch with mother earth. But a question of importance comes before us here: for very many of us the struggle is too largely on this plane of physical effort, and little energy is left when a lull comes in the battle. Life is for many of us a prolonged and often losing battle for bread and butter. But suppose for a moment that there were no longer any need for such a desperate fight; what then? If we were free from any necessity to use our physical powers as we now have to do, what would happen to us? What *does* happen to those who in our modern life are further and further removed from the earth? Something certainly goes out of their life; and no intellectual or spiritual interests can make up for this loss. Indeed, on these other levels man, as a spiritual being, is impoverished if he is cut away from his base.

In considering religion it is a fatal error to forget the body.

There are in the Pacific sunny islands where it used not to be necessary for men to struggle to win their daily food. Nature was not a miserly stepmother to them, but a doting mother. Did that condition lead to a rich development of other powers? All the evidence is to the contrary. It may well be that the cessation of struggle on the physical plane might for us, as for them, lead to deterioration. That is why they are wise who think much of leisure and of the preparation of man for the leisure which may be his in some coming age. This is in reality a preparation for him of interests and conflicts on another level to which the struggle may be transferred. What would be fatal to man would be the total cessation of conflict.

We may move from the physical to the intellectual level, but the new search there might be limited to the mysteries of this visible universe. "In nature's infinite book of secrecy" we might learn to read a little. The poets of the Elizabethan era were overwhelmed with wonder when they thought of the many mysteries of the universe that awaited discovery, and of man, who was called by something within him to enter boldly into that unknown land. They had heard from that land a voice which could be interpreted by man; they had seen a path into that land, a path which the soul of man might take.

" Our souls whose faculties can comprehend
  The wondrous architecture of the world,
  And measure every wand'ring planet's course,
  Still striving after knowledge infinite,
  And always moving as the restless spheres."

So sang Marlowe, who was deemed by his contempo-
raries a skeptic in religion. But for Marlowe, whatever
his religion might have been, it was a certainty that
between the spirit of man and this universe there was
an understanding to be sought and found. The spirit
of man might seek for the meaning of this universe
in which it was set. *Man must seek.*

Long ago in the book of Job the two levels were
described in poetry which still captures the mind of
every reader. The triumphs of man, the miner, by his
physical prowess are sung: " He setteth an end to darkness and searcheth out all perfection: the stones of
darkness and the shadow of death."

But there is another level made known to man by
the divine wisdom. There is another way which is hid
from the eyes of all living and kept closed from the
birds of the air. To that way, the way of wisdom,
man is called — the same man who wins his bread from
the earth and takes iron out of the earth. It is his
glory that, sharing this earth with the fowls of the air,
he can find a way which the vulture's eye hath not
seen. For, to seek wisdom is man's true end; until
he takes that other way which God understandeth,
and enters into this other secret, hidden from all other
creatures, he is not man at all.

Man in quest of knowledge is man giving expression to that vision which is given to him. He is the
artist who seeks to express in stone or on canvas the
thoughts of his heart. The artist, too, is a witness to
the unquenchable spirit of man. Why did he ages
ago sharpen stone and carve on the walls of his cave
the things which he had seen? There was nothing in
such drawings that could benefit his physical life. He

did not hunt any more swiftly or strike his prey more surely because he had drawn upon his screen the beasts by which he was surrounded. There may have been a trace of magic in his activity, but magic does not explain him.

Man the artist takes his material and upon it impresses his thought. He is not satisfied till he has told in all the ways open to him what is dawning upon him in the hidden and unfathomable reaches of his mind. The artist is also a seeker along ways which the vulture's eye hath not seen. Man the artist lifts the search of man the child of earth to another level. Here is the stone, hewn by the art and device of man from the earth; here is man, fed by the food which he has won from the earth, and man the thinker, with food which others knew not of. Out of these ingredients man creates art.

The world is full of monuments out of the past which tell how far man has traveled in the world invisible. Everywhere he leaves upon the earth the confessions not of his kinship with the other creatures of the earth, but of his aspiration after knowledge and of his visions of beauty which they do not know. He is the thinker and the artist. We do not say when we see monuments which man has left to the ages, " How clever his hands were! " We say, " Into what hidden worlds he had entered! "

Yet in every land and in every age he has never been able to rest content with any of his many achievements. He is always a being conscious that he belongs to another world. Almost before he knows it he finds himself on the track of Another in whose hands is his breath and whose are all his ways. He is always seen, when he is most himself, to be on the track of God.

Here it is not only helpful, it is essential, that we consider the Bible. If nothing more is granted at the outset, it is agreed that anyone who studies man on the track of God must read the Bible. Simplicity and fearless realism are found in it. Man is never treated there as a creature imprisoned in his physical life; he is always man the child of earth. When he is described in his search for God it is in nature, in history, in Christ the crucified and risen Lord, that he seeks, but he is never lifted out of nature.

Nowhere is there a more frank acceptance than in the Bible of the fact that human life has many levels. We are never far from nature there, and from nature not in the least robbed of its terrors. Indeed for some readers the very realism is a stumbling block. Those who like to ignore what they call the lower elements in man's life and are tired of what was called by the Stoic " the weary bondage to the flesh," may be offended by the frankness of these ancient books. A spade is called a spade. Man is treated not as spirit but as man. But in the present day there is less likelihood of such offense. We have returned, happily, to a healthier state of mind. We are not ashamed of Brother Ass the body, and we do not imagine that the God of the living has no concern for man except as a soul, nor that he begins to take notice of him only when he becomes " religious."

The writers of the Old Testament are never uprooted from mother earth. They always have their ear to the ground, listening to its voices; they never lose their wonder and terror in the presence of nature. We do not forget that we belong to this visible earth, and, being its children, are driven to discover all that can be known of its secrets.

In the Bible we read for the most part of a people busy upon their farms, directly dependent upon their herds and their crops, watching the sun making his journey " coming out as a bridegroom from his chamber and rejoicing as a strong man to run a race." They dreaded the havoc of the storm; they welcomed the rains which came down on the mown grass. They learned to trace Orion and the Pleiades in the midnight sky. They studied the plants of the earth from which they received herbs of healing as well as kindly fruits. They had but little of the science which we have mastered, but they had the heart of the scholars who read God's thoughts after him.

In their searching they did not separate nature from God as though there were no relation between the natural and the spiritual levels of life. The temptation of the common people in Israel was rather to consider themselves one with nature. They were indeed tempted to go the common way of all Syrian religions and to take for their gods the processes of nature, exalting them to divine honor. That was the way along which Ahab, and Jezebel who made Ahab to sin, and the priests of Baal would have led Israel. It was the one alluring alternative which drew them away from the God who had redeemed them out of Egypt. They were tempted to sink to that lower level in their search for God, to go with all the tribes of Canaan, which held that the processes of nature were the chief clues to knowledge of the Most High. This meant at best a pantheism in which all was God, at worst a deification of lust. It was not for nothing that the prophets fought to the death against the worship of the Baalim.

When they turned from the worship of Astarte, the queen of heaven, and came back to the living and holy God, they did not forget that they were children of this earth and that their God was the Maker of heaven and earth. He was the Holy God, but he was still Lord of the World. Their songs of praise to him were filled with the symbols and parables of earth and sea and sky. To this day we sing their words: " The heavens declare the glory of God."

To the seers of Israel this was God's world. They sought to know what it was like; and in all their discoveries they knew that they were on the track of something still more wonderful, beyond their utmost knowledge.

But in their search into nature they found themselves strangely held and fettered; they were in the presence of dark powers by which they were bound and held down. The realm of nature was not only a gracious world in which signals were flashed from the eternal Lord; it was also a scene haunted by dark powers with which man had to contend. Man was fettered in the world of nature. He was not free from terrors; nor did he discover, as he looked at things as they were, that nature was altogether kind or just. He was often tempted to think that the Power behind all things was unfriendly, or perhaps indifferent.

There is a needful warning in the Scriptures to those who talk in a romantic language about nature and declare that all that we need to know of God may be discovered on her level. If all that can be known of God may be seen in the processes of nature, then the verdict of our minds upon his character must be uncertain. Israel knew this; and she was guarded by the prophets from the temptation, so strongly entrenched in eastern religions, to deify nature. The prophets looked for God on the level of their physical life, but not for all that could be known of him.

And if in our search we discover that there are forces in nature which must be fought by man, and this realization troubles us, we can remind ourselves that these children of the ancient world of whom we read knew this fear also; they, too, understood what it meant to be ambushed by dark powers. As children of the earth they needed a deliverer.

But in that level of life, with all its terrors and joys, the seers of Israel found the way, as we must find it, to that other level in which they listened to the divine voice and felt the pressure of the divine hand. They were not only children of mother earth; they were lifted to the level on which they knew themselves to be the children of God. "Whom have I in heaven but Thee? And there is none upon earth I desire beside Thee." This was their cry. Beginning in the realm of nature, they were lifted above all that they could be in themselves into the realm of the spirit.

It is unlikely that our experiences will duplicate theirs in detail. But we may discover that for us too there are the same levels upon which we may look for God, and these levels are for us, as for them, not separated, nor are they complete without one another. We too must live as children of this earth, and in so living discover that we are children of eternity.

If we think of the house of life as a house with stories — a useful but clearly incomplete picture — we must not think of the stories as composed of different apartments without communication with one another. The attempt to run the departments of life as though each were completely detached from the others only ends in disaster. The man who forgets Brother Ass is inviting trouble for himself. Brother Ass is not such a fool after all. He has his revenge. And the man who, on the other hand, ignores the spirit lives in a process which has no end and is meaningless. He is a character in a tale which is broken off; his life is doomed to futility.

To illustrate these levels of life we can picture to ourselves an ancient church on a Sunday morning. We come from the countryside in the summer weather and within the cool shadows of the church we meet for worship with the village folk.

A swallow flies through the window and flutters above the altar.* In it there is life. Like all other creatures it is sensitive to stimulus. It moves; it may even be said to love and to rejoice. But if it sings praises in the church they are unconscious praises; it brings its offerings unknowingly. It seeks God as birds seek the south when autumn comes. The psalmist said that in the temple the sparrow had found her a house, and the swallow a nest where she might lay her young. In his joyful song the singer acknowledges that there is a relation between the life of the birds and the worship of the house of God.

In a very real sense the life of the swallow is linked

* Evelyn Underhill has written a beautiful poem on such a theme.

to the life of man.	Man and bird are alike creatures who live for the glory of God.	Man too is a creature of the earth; dust he is and to dust he returns.	He should not forget his humbler kindred.	Nor in his worship must he forget that other creatures are praising God with him.

There is something profoundly true in the story of St. Francis preaching to the birds.	It is a prophecy of the final unity of all creatures in God.	The pictures in which artists show the ox and the ass by the manger at Bethlehem are no less true; they show the life of the incarnate Lord as it is revealed to sentient beings and in them.	Created beings are bringing their worship, all unconscious as it may be, to the Word Incarnate.	Man is their priest; this man is the high priest of all life, for he himself has taken flesh and blood.	We may look for God on that earthly level.

But in that same church there are evidences of another level of life.	The building tells how man the maker has been able to impress his mind upon material things.	The bird builds its nest, but man has taken the stones of the earth and fashioned them into a sanctuary with a beauty of its own and a grace which make it a fitting world from man to the unseen world in the heart of which the earth is set.	Man is an artist as other creatures are not.	He lives in his art.	He has made the very stones to speak.	He has taken reeds and strings and made music.	He has written and printed books.	He has made glass catch and temper the light of the sun.	With his brush and his pigments he has recaptured stories out of a remote age.	Man lives, but not as the swallow lives.	He has arrived at another level.	He has taken hold of the material provided for him by the senses and made it serve his ends as a thinker and a maker. What is it, then, that distinguishes him from the other creatures? It is his conscious vision and his power to give it expression. He has taken a way which is hidden from other creatures. He may have arrived by almost imperceptible stages, but when he has arrived the difference is plain. On that level where man the artist works we can seek for God.

On each of his levels he reflects God. Religious people are often in danger of shutting God out of what they call the lower levels of life. They think it unworthy to look for God on these levels. They cannot believe that God can be revealed in beings who have no consciousness of him. They prefer to think of God as entering upon the scene only when mankind has reached the spiritual level and can speak with him as a friend. We find a certain satisfaction to our vanity when we suppose that God cannot be praised by any other creatures. We may come to despise our origin. We may refuse in our pride to look for God on each level where he is to be found.

For us, if such is our mind, there is a rebuke in the close of the book of Jonah. Jonah had been disappointed with God for sparing Nineveh. He himself had prophesied that Nineveh would be destroyed, but that heathen city had repented and had been spared. Jonah was humiliated; he was jealous for his own reputation as a prophet. But he had always feared that God would not be firm enough with the heathen. Jonah spoke for the nationalism in Israel which looked upon heathen cities as fuel for the fire of divine vengeance. But the Lord God teaches Jonah what

Nineveh means to him — " six score thousand persons which cannot distinguish their right hand from their left, and also much cattle." God cares for all these creatures in Nineveh; none of them can be conscious of him, but in them too his life is reflected. In the little children and even in the cattle of Nineveh Jonah could have found God.

We have no right to despise the life which all the animals share with us as though somehow our origin were something shameful which we ought to hide, and as though nothing of God's glory can be seen in anything lower than the spiritual. The Holy Scriptures do not teach us to think so. It is better to believe with the sacred writers that God has seen all these creatures and pronounced them good, and that in the life of the earth God " tastes an ancient rapture." It is better to be materialists, if by so being we can still believe that something of God is revealed in the earth and that his sacraments are there to be found, and if we see " every common bush aflame with God."

Nor need man in his office as artist and maker be set outside the life of God. God is himself an artist. Where the life of the mind expresses itself in stone or color, where the craftsman takes hold of some material and seems to tear the secret out of it, chiseling and turning to his use the stones of the earth, there also is God Almighty, there we may seek for him, for there is life, and where life is, God is. This level also reflects God's glory, and there he gives meaning to the lower level. Man who builds a church lifts with him to that level all the other created things. It is not all there is to be known of God that we find there, but only on this level shall we enter into the knowledge of his character and purpose.

Is that all there is to be found in that village church? The service begins; a new fact comes to light. Here is the spirit of man praying and in this way speaking to God. Man makes his answer to a voice which he believes has spoken to him. At the heart of this worship he is recalling the ancient story of the crucified youth by whose hands redemption has been wrought. It is an ancient story which is still alive. That crucified Lord still lives, and in him man has reached another level of his spiritual life. He walks in the heavenly places with God. The same worshiper is at once an animal who eats and drinks, a craftsman who makes things, a thinker; and now he comes to the highest level of all, that for which all life was made: he is in Christ.

It may be that for most of the worshipers that mysterious life is touched only now and then. The air is too rarefied for them to breathe at all times. They do not hold fast what they touch at intervals. But they *have* touched it, and that is a prophecy of what will be.

There are some, the called of God, who carry the intellectual gains of man to the level of the life of the spirit. The animal life — to use a rough description — is fulfilled in the intellectual, the intellectual in the life of the spirit. Man standing within eternity is the heir of God and the joint-heir of Christ. The creation in him is delivered out of the bondage of corruption into the glorious liberty of the children of God. All the levels of life are there, and all his seekings are fulfilled there.

If this is the way of life, how in the experience of man does it stand related to the life of the Word Incarnate? Surely it is realized perfectly in that one life which we, who have received life from Him, realize in a small measure.

In Christ was life. He it is who, by his life and death and his resurrection and his prolonged ministry through the Spirit, is set in the midst of our race as the revealer and the quickener of life. If we return to the church building he is there in the midst of his people, the source and sustainer of their life. Man in nature, man in history, man in Christ — there are levels of life, but all are fulfilled in the living Christ.

It comes to this. We must seek for God. But we need not limit our field to what is known as spiritual. The Christian is of all men the one permitted to be the frankest materialist. Matter to him is not outside the life of God. This world is no foreign land from which the exile longs to return home. It is in one sense a battlefield where he must win his soul, in another a mansion of God's house, in which indeed there are many mansions.

What ways, then, are opened to the seeker?

There are many ways leading into the city of man's soul. Down each of them we may go in search of God. Down each of them we may look for his coming. But not in all his grace and truth can he be seen, except in the Word Incarnate. " God who at sundry times and in divers manners spake in time past unto the fathers by the prophets, hath in these last days spoken unto us by his Son, whom he hath appointed heir of all things, by whom also he made the world."

IV

SEEKING GOD IN CHURCH

" IT IS about time," said Tom, " that we held a committee meeting of the tennis club. It won't be easy to find a time."

" I suggest," said Dick, " that we meet on Sunday morning at 11 A.M."

" That will suit me," said Harry, Jim and Joe.

" I'm sorry," said Bob, " that I can't manage it. I am going to church."

A silence followed.

" I am not quite sure that I caught that," said Tom. " It almost sounded as if he said that he was going to church."

" Do people do such things still? " asked Dick.

" They say," said Harry, " that you can hear some good music in church."

" I went myself once a long time ago," said Jim, who was twenty-one years of age, " but I'm afraid it was for reasons not directly connected with the sacredness of the occasion."

" It might relieve our anxieties," said Tom, " if this odd though far from useless member of the club would explain why he goes to church."

" I go to look for God," answered Bob.

Another silence.

" Perhaps sometime," said Tom, " you might tell

47

us why you go there to seek for God, and what you find there."

We are thinking of ways at hand in which we can look for God. If we were told of a sacred temple in the east, or of some shrine in the west, we might consider the journey. But what if a few yards away there is a place in which we may look for God? Why should we not go to church in search of him?

There must be no hiding the facts when we consider the church as it is found today. It is under fire, and in many things it deserves to be under fire. The charges leveled against it must not make the churchman angry; they are often exaggerated, prejudiced, ignorant; but it is more important to discover the measure of truth in them than to score points against the critics. Certainly the defender of the church cannot speak to this generation without shame and penitence. He should know better than the critics where it has failed. Within its own borders the church should be its own relentless critic.

Some years ago a pageant was written by Laurence Housman for St. Martin's-in-the-Fields. It presented in a series of historical episodes the story of the church since the day when St. Martin divided his cloak with the beggar. It was not the glorious scenes only that were shown. The shame of the church was not hidden, but openly confessed. The last scene was placed in Hyde Park. A communist orator was denouncing in scornful words the failure of the church to witness to the spirit of brotherhood. The final word was with the witness, who throughout the pageant commented on the scenes. This was not a word of anger or bitter denial, but rather the answer of a society which knows and confesses with shame its sins against its calling. What had been said by its critic was unjust and unbalanced; but how far was it true?

Let it be admitted that as likely as not the church to which we go in search of God will be very human in its imperfections. We must not go in search of a perfect church, but we can keep before us the things which are essential.

Almost the first condition for those who seek in the church for God is that they lay aside their fastidiousness. Good people often mistake refinement for holiness. They do not like " common people," and by that they mean people whose manners and appearance are displeasing to them. They almost take it for granted that in the kingdom of heaven there will be room only for nice people. They may even be heard to commend their own local church on the ground that there are very nice people there.

Nothing can be clearer from the records of the gospel than that our Lord did not associate with nice people only. He was accused of being a friend of publicans and sinners, and at one time it looked as if he had a special mission to publicans. No one who lived in Corinth ever supposed that the followers of the Way were nice people. Some were, and gave themselves airs about it, but others were mean and contemptible in the eyes of the Corinthians. They were, as St. Paul admitted, nobodies.

Those who seek for God must not be superior in their judgments or think that they are on a level above that on which these ordinary people move. There was no more learned scholar of our time than Baron von

Hügel. In one of his books he uses an illustration from the saintly life of a poor woman with whom he had the honor of being a fellow worshiper in a Midland church. The reference in the index, filled as it is with names of learned men, is significant: " Washerwoman, the, p. —." In that humble life what did the scholar find? He would not have hesitated to say that he found God.

And why should we be so superior? What are we but human beings, born of the same family as the others — sharing in a common human inheritance of sin and failure, of sorrow and sickness and pain, of love that quickens and wounds; heirs of a common life moving swiftly to the universal experience of death?

In a letter to his niece this same profound thinker gave some wise counsel. His niece had written to him of the dullness of the country church services. He replied:

The touching, entrancing beauty of Christianity, my niece, depends upon a subtle something which all this fastidiousness ignores. Its greatness, its special genius, consists, as much as in anything else, in that it is without this fastidiousness. A soul that is, I do not say tempted, but dominated, by such fastidiousness, is as yet only hovering round the precincts of Christianity, but it has not entered its sanctuary, where heroism is always homely, where the best always acts as a stimulus toward helping toward being (in a true sense) but one of the semi-articulate, bovine, childish, repulsively second-third-fourth-rate crowd. . . . It is, really, a very hideous thing; the full, truly free beauty of Christ alone completely liberates us from this miserable bondage.

If we make the condition that we shall go to church on the understanding that we shall find only educated, refined, pleasant people, we shall enter it in vain. We have no business to seek those only; and if we did we should not find them. The people we shall find in church will be of all ages and of all sorts and conditions. Some will be tired, holding on to their churchmanship only out of habit. Some will be quick, others slow in their understanding. Some will be pleasant and interesting, others, as we say at first sight, stuffy and dull. They will have sharp differences and perhaps quarrels. The preacher may or may not be a master of the art, the perilous art, of preaching. The choir may be good or bad. A good choir may sing bad music, and a bad choir may murder good music. And the societies which are at work within the larger compass of the church may also be of all kinds — some with little attraction for the mind of youth, some merely survivals of a day of enthusiasm long ended, some that have been a long time in dying. At least it will not be denied that a visitor to the many churches which are found in the cities and villages of any country will find some which do not offer a promising way for the seeker after God.

But no society ought to be judged in the sweeping way in which the church is judged. Almost everybody seems to think himself qualified to pronounce a sweeping judgment on this society. Generalizations are hastily made on the basis of a very small experience. It is not hard to find men who have done with the church because of some slight which they met with years ago in their local church. It is almost a daily experience to hear men speak of what the *church* teaches, what mistakes the *church* has made, how the *church* ought to mend its ways.

Now the church should not be condemned by anyone who has not made some attempt to discover what it stands for when it is true to its own calling. Before it is condemned it might be in order to inquire what our life would be like without the church even as it is today.

In his pageant " The Rock," * T. S. Eliot set himself to defend those who in our modern cities build temples for the worship of God and in them bear witness before men to the Light Invisible. He describes the life of a modern suburb:

" A CRY FROM THE NORTH, from the WEST and from the
    SOUTH
  WHENCE THOUSANDS TRAVEL DAILY TO THE TIME KEPT
    CITY:
  Where My Word is unspoken,
  In the land of lobelias and tennis flannels
  The rabbit shall burrow and the thorn revisit.
  The nettle shall flourish on the gravel court,
  And the wind shall say: ' Here were decent godless
    people:
  Their only monument the asphalt road
  And a thousand lost golf-balls.' "

If we think of such a land, and then in our imagination try to understand what a house of God would

* In *Collected Poems* (Faber and Faber).

mean there, we shall not be so swift to condemn the very imperfect societies which do at least keep before the eyes of men the light of God, and do offer to them the Word and the sacraments by which alone human life can be raised to its true glory. They may do this most faultily, but they are the only societies that do it at all.

At least there is a church to be explored by us. We shall be foolish if in our search for God we neglect a society which by its history and in its worship does exist for this very thing, to perpetuate and to offer to mankind a way to God. Therefore it must be said in all frankness to those who are seeking God that they must not pass by the door of the church on the ground that it is the home of a motley crowd of people who fall far short of their calling.

Nor is it fair to claim that if the Lord of the church were there, and not these his poor followers, we should be ready to enter those sacred buildings. Should we? Are we sure that we are ready to face his judgment? Would he be so easy with us? Would he meet us in a reasonable way?

It is conceivable too that he may be there even now. Others in an hour like that through which we are passing have found in the sanctuary a way that was a right way and that led them to God, not a track that was lost.

There is a story of one such seeker in the Psalms. Some of these hymns, which were arranged for the second temple, carry within them records of personal adventures and hairbreadth escapes. This particular story is so fitted to our own spiritual condition that it might have been written yesterday.

The seeker of the story had almost lost hope. " As for me, my feet were well-nigh gone." Like another poet in a later age he had almost yielded up all moral questions in despair. He could not make sense of this world, viewed as he had to view it as God's world. Everywhere evil was exalted, everywhere the good cast down; and where in all this scene was God? He could see no way out of the last fear of all — the fear that God did not take any interest in the affairs of man. That was always the dread which startled the Hebrew when he woke in the night. That is the last fear which chills us still. This seeker was more troubled about God than he was about man. How would the character of God emerge in history? He went over the facts; he arranged them and rearranged them, he changed a little here and there; but the problem always worked out to the same answer. Perhaps God did not know, or perhaps he knew and did not care. Either way the prospect was dark.

Then he went into the sanctuary. He was desperate; in his search for an answer he went, as we should put it, to church. The temple for him was not unlike church as we know it. There were within its walls the same men and women we find today, subject to the same passions, weak, tempted, with minds distracted, sometimes fearing man more than they feared God. A fastidious saint could despise them as he can now, but not a desperate man.

There in the temple would be symbols which told as much or as little as symbols tell us today of what God had done for his people and what his holy and eternal purpose was. Words which we still repeat

were on the lips of men in that temple. They were
words familiar in the daily life of men. How otherwise could any message from an unseen world come
through to the human mind? Not in any strange
tongue could God speak to man.

It was as a desperate man that the singer went into
the sanctuary. It was a last resort. Desperate men
cannot be choosers. He expected little, but he was not
the first nor the last to try this way. He went into
the temple in one mind; he came out in another.
What had come to him? It is not easy to put into
exact language, but it was certainly the provision of
new facts, and with them of a new point of view from
which to look at the old facts. These new facts had
everything to do with the sanctuary. They were
not a set of arguments such as a lawyer might set
forth as he opens a case. It was more a new level
of thought and feeling to which he was lifted than a
new statement of the evidence. But it made all the
difference to him. He sought something that the
new experience had given to him, something which
was far beyond all the needs of the bitter hour through
which he was passing.

> " Nevertheless I am still with Thee.
> Thou hast holden me by my right hand;
> I am Thine."

He became very sure of God, and of a God who did
not solve his problems but gave himself to his child.
" I am *with* thee." That was enough to make that
sanctuary shine with an eternal radiance. The seeker
did not find a defense of his theology; he found God.

Let us leave that temple to take our place in a modern city, and think of such a man in these days going to church.

His feet too have "well-nigh slipped." He reads in the papers of poor and feeble tribes robbed of their inheritance by grasping nations. He hears of those who grow rich by cruel measures and are proud; and "their tongue walketh through the earth," or, as we might say, their words have an international importance on all the bourses of the world. He is himself out of work and suffers from lack of food. He fought in the World War, but not having been numbered among the heroes who fell he is now not so much a hero as a nuisance. He watches the herds of men rushing or being driven like the swine of the Gadarenes down a steep place into the sea. And what does God care?

Then he goes to church. He too goes as a desperate man clinging with a feeble hold to the faith of his childhood. The church into which he goes is not in any way remarkable either for its beauty or its ritual. It is one of a thousand such churches. The worshipers within it are as motley a company as they were in the temple of old. The preacher is not an eloquent man nor a spiritual giant; he is one of tens of thousands of honest and hard-working ministers of the gospel who can be found in any country. The Sacred Book is read, hymns are sung, prayers are offered, the sermon is preached. Or it may be the holy communion is celebrated. Nothing but the customary traditional forms of worship. There are no signs of enthusiasm. It is not a time of revival, but one of the long periods between those hours.

Yet in such a place something new is given to him. It is not that the preacher delivers a sermon on the problem of evil in the world or upon the wrongs which Christian people should challenge. It is certainly not because any new facts are brought before him. But none the less something is given to him which provides fresh hope for him. For it is the hope to be found in the church which impresses the visitor more than anything else. There are many words which speak of sorrow and the shadow of death. But the total impression is one not of gloom but of confidence and hope. In the world, it was promised, there would be tribulation, but there are said to be some who have overcome the world. The hope that this may be his experience is created by the working together of many forces.

Such a visitor could not enter a church without remembering that its very existence is a startling fact. Here in the heart of a modern city is a building sacred to the memory of one Jesus of Nazareth, a Jewish teacher whom some declared to be Son of God. He had died on the cross more than nineteen hundred years ago. So far as the greater number of those who had known him were concerned, he was last seen a dead man nailed to a cross in the company of two other dead men. Yet in a modern city in this present day there are still those who for some reason remember this strange man. They do not think of him as a dead hero. Why should a dead hero be remembered as Christ is remembered in the holy communion, by the eating of bread and the drinking of wine? This young Prince of Glory, as one of their hymns calls him, was in some way a living Saviour whose name is

still precious.   Still they are singing, " Jesus, thou joy
of loving hearts. . . ." Of what dead hero can this be
said?

Things which have become precious are not easily
laid aside.   Man has a pathetic desire to keep alive
the great souls who have given themselves for their
friends.   But why should a number of modern men
and women meet in the name of such a dead hero,
read translations from ancient books about him, sing
hymns of adoration to him and utter words which
speak of their nourishment by his broken body and
his blood which was shed?   The presence of the church
of Christ in modern society is a startling fact, not the
less startling if it is noted how ordinary are the people
within it.   Only our familiarity with it blinds us to the
miracle that is before our eyes in the very presence of
this ancient society.

But why should we seek the Redeemer among these
ordinary men and women?   This criticism is made
everywhere.   Sometimes it is joined to a request that
we seek him in the church invisible.   We need not be
bound down to this poor imperfect society but, it is
said, should rather seek our home in the perfected city
of God.

It is common to say that men do not believe in
organized religion.   This means, in other words, that
we do not believe in the only church which we can
hope to find.   We are now living in a world of time
and space.   We have to do with particular things and
persons.   We do not shape our life by our relations
with man, nor do we spend our days on some undefined and unsearchable region called earth.   We live

with certain individual human beings; we have a little piece of this earth on which we are at home. If our religion is to be of any service to us in such a life it must appeal to us not as though we were above or out of this scene and already in some invisible world; it must come to us as we are at this moment. If we were other than we are we might have a philosophy, but it is not philosophy we seek but God, and God cannot be known to us except as he becomes incarnate.

But we cannot accept this faith without facing other inevitable conclusions. The Lord made flesh must live still in his body, and that body must be a human society. What is the church but the body of Christ? And it is not the less his body in that it consists of weak and faltering men and women still fighting against their temptations and often fighting a losing battle.

Among such mortals if anywhere we must look for the living Christ. Not in the heavens above, but here. He is not to be separated from his body. And when we speak of Christian people as his body we mean not simply that they need his wisdom and love and power to throb through them, but also that he needs them; he is not to be separated from them. To despise the church of Christ and to set our whole affection on an invisible church of the saints in glory is to be disloyal to the Lord Christ.

We must seek for God in his church on earth. There he has pledged himself to meet us.

V

CAN WE SEEK HIM IN THE DARKNESS?

Yea though I walk through the valley of the shadow of death I will fear no evil, for Thou art with me.

NO MAN can hope to find God if he deliberately blinds himself to the dark facts of this human scene and chooses to live only in the world of pleasant things, chatting of all that is disquieting as though it existed only in a tale. No man can come to walk in the light of God unless he is prepared in the service of truth to walk also in the darkness. It is not ours to choose the darkness; but if the way lies through it we must arise and go, or lose our souls. If God will have us to go by green pastures and still waters we shall accept his will. If he will lead us into the valley of the shadow of death thither also we must go. We must not decide beforehand by which discipline he shall prepare us for our place in his eternal kingdom.

You can find God in the darkness. You can find also in the darkness a way to his kingdom. There may come an hour in which for the sake of his loyalty to truth a man has to enter into the darkness of doubt and even of complete unbelief. Such experiences have often come to men in times in which new discoveries were made — when, for example, Copernicus compelled men to look to the heavens with startled eyes, or when Darwin made men think afresh on the problem of the origin of species. When such times come they " test men's souls." Some have said in such hours, with the flippancy which may go with an outward piety, " Let us hope it is not true, but if it is true let us hush it up." But others were not prepared to ignore the new hypotheses and the facts which were proved in support of them. On the one side there stretched the old familiar road with the familiar light, tender and sacred, resting upon it; on the other, a steep way leading down to the dark valley. They seemed to themselves to be saying farewell to their former faith and to be losing the light of their hope forever, but they had no other way. They knew that " he who begins by loving Christianity better than truth will proceed by loving his own sect or church better than Christianity, and end in loving himself better than all." * This is literally true, though when the decisive choice is made the man does not know it. For the sake of truth, since he is compelled as its sworn soldier to obey its call, he may lose his faith; but though he suffer long, not by loyalty to truth will he lose the God who desires truth in the inward parts. There is a price to be paid in the revelation of truth to man, and that price may be the loss for a time of the vision of God.

There never was an age in which so many were compelled to adjust their traditional belief to new facts as are so compelled today. Choices which in ancient times or in the Middle Ages had to be made by the few are now to be made by a large number. The dissemination to all of information through printing

* S. T. Coleridge.

press and radio forces the average man to make decisions, the man who in other ages was left to carry on undisturbed the old traditions. It might have been fantastic in those times to warn such men that they might be called to enter into the region of twilight and perhaps of darkness. It is not fantastic today. Things which were once whispered are now shouted abroad. Boys in the sixth form or boys in a senior Sunday school are busy upon problems which were once considered out of their range. It is said that the undergraduate of today knows as much as did the graduate of some years ago.

There are dangers here. Choices may have to be made upon a hasty or imperfect summary of the facts. It is easy for a fearless student to say that astronomy, geology, biology, history and now psychology have robbed the Christian church of one line of defense after another, and the honest man has now to start there — with the ground clear of the old religion. But no man does any service to truth by a reckless acceptance of untested " facts." The loyal servant of the truth knows that he must be loyal in the search for truth as well as in the service of truth when he has found it.

The story of Romanes, the famous biologist of the late Victorian era, is familiar to those who belonged in their youth to the same age. His name lives in the Romanes Lecture which is delivered annually in Oxford.

The eclipse of faith came to him in the course of a steadfast following of truth; all who knew him counted him among the pure in heart to whom it is promised that they shall see God. " He had always cared more for truth," it was said of him, " for the knowledge of God, than for anything else in the world." In the loyalty to truth which his study of science demanded, he lost his faith. He lived in the age in which Charles Darwin, his master and friend, by his *Origin of Species* brought to the knowledge of men certain new facts which no serious student could ignore. To many the new teaching threatened the very existence of theism. Some defenders of the faith did not help such scientific students as Romanes. With sad and reluctant backward glances he went into the darkness. He became an agnostic and for a time almost a materialist. He knew the price that he was paying. To him the loss of faith was no light matter.

> I am not ashamed to confess that with this virtual negation of God the universe to me has lost its soul of loveliness; and although from henceforth the precept to work " while it is day " will doubtless but gain an intensified force from the terribly intensified meaning of the words that " the night cometh when no man can work," yet when at times I think, as think at times I must, of the appalling contrast between the hallowed glory of that creed which once was mine and the lonely mystery of existence as now I find it, at such times I shall ever feel it impossible to avoid the sharpest pang of which my nature is capable.

These words were written while he was under the eclipse which he did not know to be only an eclipse.

But he did not turn back; and in the darkness there came to him, not in a moment, but slowly and painfully, the certainty of the truth of the Christian faith.

In 1878 he would have rejected as impossible any idea of a return to faith. When he died in 1894 he had come back to his faith and had defended it. His life in the years of eclipse was to all appearances one of happiness and even of mirth, but he never lost his sorrow and his longing. Always he was loyal to the facts as they came to him, and in particular to the stubborn facts, and through that loyalty, that " endurance of incompleteness," he was led back to the faith which was his joy in youth:

> The sincerely scientific mind shows such tenacity as that under every trial of its faith and patience, howsoever long and unpromising and unrelieved; for it knows itself responsible not for attainment, but for perseverance: not for conquest but for loyalty.*

In that patience he won his soul.

In a poem written near the end of his life Romanes sang his *nunc dimittis*, in which he likened himself to one of the aliens militant sojourning on earth. These were his words to his Lord whom he had found again after many days:

" As thou hast found me ready to thy call,
  Which stationed me to watch the outer wall,
  And, quitting joys and hopes that once were mine,
  To pace with patient steps this narrow line,
  Oh! may it be that, coming soon or late,
  Thou still shalt find thy soldier at the gate

---

  * Ethel Romanes, *The Life of Romanes* (Longmans, Green and Co., Ltd.), p. 353.

Who then will follow thee till sight needs not to
    prove,
And faith will be dissolved to knowledge of thy love."

He came to know who had set him there; but even in
the dark years when he did not know this he was still
one of God's soldiers pacing that wall. God's soldiers!
The soldier does not decide where his post must be.

Yet it was in that darkness he found what he had
lost, and found it a more wonderful and satisfying
treasure than he had known it before. We can at least
be certain that the man who came through that darkness because he had been loyal to truth and fearless
in the search for it and because he had kept back none
of the price demanded of him, was worthy to be called
one of the sons of God. If he had turned back to the
sunnier ways he might have escaped much sorrow, but
would he have found what he did find?

There is a suspicion abroad that men come to the
dilemma where they must choose between God and
truth, and that in blinding themselves to truth they
may be winning favor with God. That this is blas-
phemous everyone can see who gives it a moment's
thought; that it is impossible we should see no less
clearly. "Things are what they are, and the conse-
quences will be what they will be."

But it is not always admitted that in the Bible itself is the vindication of those who challenge the darkness and in time, it may be long or short, find their
way to God.

The choice may come at any time to the man who
is thinking his way through the facts on which he is

compelled to form his judgment of the meaning of things. He too in the presence of new data may have to rethink his inherited religion. He too may be driven out of its shelter down strange and haunted ways. Hardest fate of all, he may be condemned as a traitor to the faith which he never desired more than in the hour in which he lost it. But he may take comfort in the remembrance that the way of the Lord Christ was not prepared only by those who found God in the sunshine, but also by men of sorrows who in their loyalty to truth were prepared to enter into the shadow of death.

The reader of the Bible, if he reads it in the right way, will find that the Lord who speaks to him there is not one whose chosen servants are expected to dissemble or to hide from him their doubts and fear. They are encouraged to speak out their minds, " to stand on their feet like men " and hold converse with him. Those of them who use the language of reproach or even despair are not reproached by their Lord; those who enter the darkness are not forgotten by him.

If we think of this very " endurance of incompleteness," which was the secret of Romanes, we shall find that it is the secret of Job. In that story every man who has to enter the darkness that comes between the old interpretation of life, which has proved inadequate, and the new, which has not yet been found, can discover himself. He is Job, and his problem is, in the heart of it, the same as Job's. Patience like that of the patriarch must be the readiness at all costs to be true to facts and to endure incompleteness. Such patience has still the same reward.

Job is the patriarch whose life, unknown to him, is of interest in the courts of heaven. But the prologue which deals with that heavenly scene is hidden from him. He is a man stripped of all things and tempted at the last to curse God and die. But the tragedy of his life lies less in the physical agonies than in the loss of the certainty of God which others knew. They believed in an order of justice, complete and undeviating. He could no longer believe this, and he had nothing to put into its place.

No book in the Old Testament makes a more instant appeal to men of our time, and no book deserves to be more carefully studied by those who are uprooted and homeless. The book is concerned with one man; it had, no doubt, its bearing upon the nation of Israel in its sorrows, but it is of Job the patriarch, " shipwrecked upon the will of God," we have to think chiefly.

God, it would appear, the only God of whom he had any knowledge, had failed him. What could he now do? Deny the facts as they had been brought home to him? Blindly affirm that the old tradition with which these facts were inconsistent was nevertheless true? His friends pleaded with him in glorious poetry not to leave the old way. There at least, with all the uncertainties that lay upon them like clouds, there were gleams of light. The other way led to darkness. In the night man wanders with no landmarks.

Few men can have passed through life without asking the question which Job asked. What was the meaning of his sufferings? They were not penalty for sin on his part; Job throughout maintains that this

explanation does not account for his sufferings. But
what then did they mean? In language of sublime
beauty and of fearless honesty Job describes his lot.
But he is more concerned for the character of God
than for any suffering which he has to bear. He
dreads this above all things, that God should be in
reality what he seems to be at that moment — a
celestial giant making his sport with a human life.

He has left the sunny places in which God's lamp
shone about him. He has left also the twilight lands
on which some dying gleams of that light could rest.
He goes bravely into the valley of the shadow of
death. He does not stop short of the last cry of faith,
" Though He slay me, yet will I trust in Him."

In the end there was restored to him the vision of
a God greater and more mysterious than any he had
known in his happier days. If it was only in gleams
he saw the promise of a restored hope, he *did* see it.
Job had endured the intervening stage in which the
old unquestioned belief is gone and the new has not
yet come. But in that stage he had found peace —
peace in the very mystery of God, so far beyond his
grasp, so remote from him, and yet so near. He came
to the place where all that a man can do is to bow in
adoration at the feet of God. " I had heard of Thee
with the hearing of the ear, but now mine eye seeth
Thee; wherefore I abhor myself in dust and ashes."

There are others in that ancient story who are called
into the darkness, not by their own personal experiences but by the sorrows of their nation. They would
gladly cling to a faith in the divine love, but they see
a world in which God seems to do nothing. They

cannot reconcile the world as they know it with a belief in the justice and mercy of the eternal God. They
are compelled to cry out to him in their bitterness of
spirit, " O Lord, thou hast deceived me and I was deceived." It was through one into whose soul this fear
had entered deeply that, in the life of Israel, the high-
way led to the cross.

Jeremiah found the road of life narrowed down to
a path, a strait way which led him into the valley of
the shadow of death. If he had shared in his youth
the hopes of the reformers among his people, he suffered the fate of all youthful reformers. He saw the
store of enthusiasm running low. Reformations are
always threatened not only by the resistance of old
vested interests but also by the defects of our human
nature, which soon grows weary and cannot hold to
the level which it has won. Jeremiah had to face the
closing of one way of hope after another. At last
nothing was left but the road, with its darkening shadows, which leads into the valley of death. His nation
must die and he must share its death; for exile to a true
Israelite meant death. And Jerusalem itself must be
left no longer the city of the great King, the virgin
daughter of Zion, but a place of death.

Yet Jeremiah, though he faltered, did not go back.
He cried aloud against his call; he used language which
on other lips would have seemed blasphemy; but when
he was called he went. And in walking that way he
began to see for himself, and for all men, what might
be the divine meaning of suffering and death. In the
thick darkness he saw a look on the face of God which
cannot be seen in the light of day. The man of sorrows looked, if it was only for a moment, upon the

face of a God who could give to a people despoiled, and even destroyed, a word which he could never have given to that same people in the proud days of David and Solomon. If today we believe that God is one who in all our sorrows has his share, we can trace the way of our faith back to the faith of Jeremiah.

What can a reader of this age expect to learn from such a prophet? He can scarcely spare time, unless he is a scholar, for the history of Jerusalem. Apart from the great voices which we hear in Jerusalem its records can have a value only to specialists in one branch of ancient history. What will be asked by such a reader is this: There is much offered to us by men of the past who have claimed to be the hearers of some divine word. Clearly such a word can come to men only by ways difficult and almost inaccessible. There may be a divine face looking upon man, but how is he to see it? There may be a voice speaking, but who will teach him the language? Here, however, is one of those rare beings who, by virtue of his place in history and also by virtue of the surrender of himself and the denial of himself, is marked out to see the heavenly vision and to hear the voice. What, then, did he see? What fresh expression on that divine face? What words did he hear such as others had not heard? What words did he understand which others had failed to understand?

These are things which a reader has a right to ask. And the answer comes that God did indeed speak to him, but God was able to speak to him because he had not turned back from the darkness. He accepted the dark lot of his people, and though this might mean the loss of all his early hopes and all the traditional beliefs of his nation, he accepted it in faith. If God would have him to be in the light, blessed be his name! If he would have him to be in the darkness, blessed also be his name!

There is yet one other who went into the darkness and saw upon that hidden face a look which others had not seen. He lived in the exile by which Israel had been broken in fragments. But the doom rested not only upon the false and faithless members of the nation, but even more upon the few, the remnant, who had never lost their faith. Why did *they* suffer? Was there any reason which could bring hope to them? Or had God cast them off forever?

In such an hour there was a prophet who entered for his people into the thick darkness where God was. In the solemn ritual of the temple the high priest entered for his people into the holy of holies. When he vanished behind the parted veil it was as if the whole congregation had gone with him. When this prophet dared in the secret of his soul to enter the darkness, he went as the representative of Israel, the new inner Israel, which now in the wreck of the old nation might be the instrument of God. For them he listened for the word of God. And what was that word but the revelation that Israel, broken, with all its earthly hopes shattered, with no earthly pride left, was called in its sorrow and suffering to bring healing to the nations; wounded for their transgressions, bruised for their iniquities, it would give its life a ransom for many.

We come here, as Christian readers have always known, within sight of the cross. It is there that this prophecy was fulfilled. But already the prophet had dared to link his own insight into the meaning of suffering with the mind of God. For there is a look of recognition in the face of the God whom the prophet sees in the darkness:

> " Would I suffer for him that I love?
> So wilt thou, so dost thou."

Did those prophecies in Isaiah concerning the servant of God who was bruised for our iniquities come to a prophet who had escaped from the darkness which fell upon his people? Could such a word have come to one who had not been prepared to enter into the deepest sorrows of his people? Not indeed to observers and onlookers could such a vision come. It could come only in the darkness.

If there are times when the burden of this sorrowful world rests heavily upon us and all our former hopes lie in the dust, when there is nothing for us but to leave the sunlit ways and enter into the darkness, then we need not think that we are leaving the God in whom we once believed. We may lose him for a time in order that we may have him forever.

You can find God. You can find him in the darkness. There may come times when you can find him there and nowhere else.

VI

THE PLAIN MAN SEEKING HELPERS

"RELIGION is what the individual does with his own solitariness." * This truth ought never to be forgotten. We shall not find God unless we are willing to face the terrors as well as the wonders and joys of the solitary life. Our Lord left us in no doubt upon this matter. "But thou when thou prayest enter into thine inner chamber and there pray to thy Father which seeth in secret." "What we make of our solitariness" belongs to the heart of all religious experience.

Our Lord himself never seems to have been far from crowds during the daytime. It is surprising to read in the Gospels how swiftly a great multitude assembled. "Straightway" there is a crowd at hand. But he knew the solitude in which "man is least alone." In the hour of his temptation he withdrew into the desert, and often when the night came he withdrew to the mountains to be alone. In the wilderness the battle was fought to a finish in solitude. There the last victory was won. Jesus died alone. By what he made of his solitariness we have been redeemed.

Let that be taken as truth, and truth of the first importance; and then let this also be added as no less true, that we need not be without helpers in our re-

* A. N. Whitehead.

ligious life. By what we make of our company, we also determine what our religion will be. Our Lord told men that they could receive help from one another. It is characteristic of him that he sent his disciples out two and two; for two are more than twice one. He promised vision and resources to those who met in fellowship, " to the two or three gathered in His name." Near the end of his earthly life, this solitary Saviour gave thanks to his disciples because they had been with him in his temptations. There could have been no memory of the Lord to move the hearts of his friends like this. *With him — in his temptations!* They were weak and faltering disciples, but he was grateful to them. *To them!* If in Gethsemane he was alone, that was not his choice. The three disciples might have watched with him, but they slept.

" The heavenly company watched while Jesus wept,
    The men he chose to share his secret slept."

Jesus did not think that his disciples should be without the confidence and insight and patience which come from the friendship of others.

Here it should be made plain once more that provision is made in the gospel not for rare spiritual beings nor for intellectual giants, but for man in every grade of his powers.

It is taken for granted that the reader of this book does not think of himself as unlike other men; they and he are not given much to thinking upon those profound studies which engage the mind of philosophers. If they are thinking of them they do not know it; they are like M. Jourdain, who had been talking prose all his life but without knowing it. They are theologians without knowing it. They are not great readers; they do not travel far in the realm of litera- ture. They do not meet often with learned men. They take the eight-thirty A.M. to town and return by the five-thirty P.M. They have their own homes and, if they are lucky, a garden to which they give some of their leisure. For a fortnight each year they go to the sea. Their friends call in the evening to have a chat. They discuss the government with a clear view of its virtues or faults. They go to church, though not as regularly as their fathers did. When they are mar- ried and have children of their own, they are glad that the youngsters should be taught the truths of religion in Sunday school. Where in such a life is there an opportunity to look for God, if they may find him? They may give up the very idea of such a search and settle down to what they call their " practical affairs."

It is idle to tell a man of this type that St. Augustine looked for God and found him after a long pilgrimage. He is not an Augustine. When he has listened in church or by the radio to the words of the mystics, he likens them to the poetry of Shelley or Keats. They are reports from a world in which he is not at home. It is a strange land with a language of its own, which means nothing to him. If he is to find God it must be within his own field of experience. There or no- where!

If we deny to such men the reward of finding God we are making a serious charge against the character and purpose of God. We are saying that he is One who can certainly be found, but only by the wise and learned and privileged; he is out of the reach of Mr. Average Man. We have read of the Celestial Surgeon and of the Comedian of the Heavens, but this would be a Celestial Snob who hides himself from all but the choice spirits and receives at his court only the most carefully selected mortals. There have even been mortals who have played the part of a lord chamberlain, carefully selecting those who can be presented at such a court.

By the conditions of their life, it is true, average people are unable to see the afterglow of the sunset on the Alps, or to hear the breakers on the coral reefs of the Pacific. They may say, as John Smith of Harrow said, " The first thing I mean to do when I get to heaven is to go to Switzerland." But if in the supreme quest of all they are shut out now from all possibility of finding the reward which God is said to offer to those who diligently seek him, then they have just cause to condemn the order in which they live. If it is for scholars alone to find him, they are cut off from the search. If they are to master the Bible as scholarship interprets it, they are cut off; they cannot hope in a crowded life to make time for that study.

If God is to be found at all, he must be found by that man, who goes by the eight-thirty A.M., and deals all day with men in business, and comes back by the five-thirty P.M., tired and worried, to his home. Can he find God?

Even the teachers of the church may forget this ordinary man in the ordinary ways of his life. They may despair of him and settle down to the dark fact that their teaching will appeal only to the few elect spirits, and for the rest all that can be done is to render a little first aid. But they should take it as a first charge upon them to offer to every man in the everyday life the good news of God, not with any thought of taking him out of that everyday life but rather with the certainty that in that life he may have communion with God.

Some of his hearers were called by our Lord to rise up and follow him. Others were sent back to their homes, there in the familiar surroundings, where everybody knew them, to declare what God had done for them. The Lord of the church chose some to be with him in the new ways, but he did not think of the others who stayed where they were as outside his kingdom.

There are Christians of many grades of knowledge and sanctity. It is no part of the Christian faith to deny a place for ambition in the spiritual life. The instinct which found expression in coveting has to be turned to a nobler use. The Christian still covets, but he covets other things. "*Covet earnestly the best gifts.*" But this is not to draw an inner circle of holy men and women, expert in the spiritual life, and to shut out the rest in an outer circle. There is always an inner Buddhism, and even Islam has had mystics with an interpretation of their faith from which the common believers were excluded. There have been some who have tried to introduce an inner Christianity, but they have never received the sanction of the Christian church.

When Pascal had that experience which is called his second conversion, he saw in the fire which shone upon him not the God of the wise and the philosophers, but "the God of Abraham, Isaac and Jacob" — the God of human folk not troubled about deep problems of thought but busy with their flocks and herds. Pascal was a genius; but in his moment of vision, when God found him, he took his place with every man.

It is for the average man that help must be sought. It is not enough to leave him in his own solitariness nor to provide him with books nor even with the great and wonderful mystery, the church. He needs something more personal. How is he in the ordinary ways of his life to seek for God? Are there any helpers waiting?

It is in the realm of personal relationships that we must look for such help. In the gospel man is as clearly treated as a social being as in the teachings of philosophers and sages. Our Lord never dealt with man as though he were a being who could live a complete life outside such relationships. Robinson Crusoe on his island, before Friday entered into his life, was not prevented by his solitude from living a Christian life. But our Lord did not provide a way of life for Robinson Crusoes. Such a man had no opportunity either of giving to others or of receiving from them, and he lived therefore a life less than complete, less even than human. He could not grow as others grow from all that they owe to their company. He could live such a life in memory and in hope; but that is not enough. In personal relationships we come to ourselves. There is something essentially Christian in the doctrine of Confucius, who recognized the five relationships in which life must be lived, those between old and young, parent and child, ruler and minister, husband and wife, elder and younger brother. Within such an order man must shape his conduct. There if anywhere he must find himself. There also he can find God.

" Or what man is there of you who, if his son ask bread, will he give him a stone? "

" For this cause shall a man leave his father and his mother, and shall cleave unto his wife."

" No man can serve two masters."

" Render unto Caesar the things that are Caesar's."

In such words our Lord laid a supreme importance upon the relations in human life between persons.

The question then arises: Can the average man, if he seeks to find God, discover any helper among the human beings to whom in some of the familiar ways of life he is related? The evidence is convincing that he can.

If there is one book in which the solitary life is set forth it is *Pilgrim's Progress*. But in that same book the pilgrim finds many to whom he owes his very soul.

When Christian set out from the City of Destruction he soon fell into the Slough of Despond, and there he might have remained floundering if a King's officer whose name was Help had not come to his aid. He it was who pointed out the steps by means of which Christian arrived at the other side. And Help was but one of many of the King's officers on the Way.

It is no part of our search for God that we should despise such royal officers. We may think that it is a finer thing to stand alone and be quite self-sufficient. We may misuse certain great truths — this, for example, that no man can come between our souls and God. That saying is true if it is rightly interpreted, but it may become a misleading fiction. If Help came between Christian and God, it was as when an appointed instrument comes between the user of it and the other who gave it. Help was between the pilgrim and the rest of the journey and the Celestial City, but only as an escort appointed by the Lord of that country; not a deputy for him, but a guide who was a minister of peace, one in whom and through whom the King of Christian's seeking came to his aid.

It is necessary to use plain words on this matter. Many men come to see late, too late in life, how much they would have gained if in some earlier day they had sought the help of others, help which was freely offered to them. Whether in their studies, or in their activities in the service of the church or the city or the nation, they could have been saved much waste of energy and been able to make much more of themselves if they had not confused self-sufficiency and self-respect, and magnified their pride into the virtue of independence.

There is an area in our life in which we say that we are self-sufficient. There, at least, we are alone. At the last, " I " — that real " I " — must say the last word. But there are many lines of communication between that " I " and others, and we should be foolish not to use them.

This is how the case may be put to a would-be seeker. You wish to find God in the realities of your life. You are not the first to seek for him. You have within your circle of friends others who have learned something on the way. They are willing to put their resources at your disposal. Why not use them? If you proposed to travel in Central Africa and a man who had been over at least some of the ground offered to tell you of his journeys, to show you his maps, to give you valuable warnings of dangers, would you not be senseless to declare that you must win your own way and start where others started? No man must come between you and that unknown land! But why not?

This is a counsel which those whose life is now largely in the past can give with authority to others: Do not be too proud to seek and to accept help. One of the noblest of all Christian men in the last generation, Bishop Westcott, at the end of a long life said, "Again and again I have lost the help of sympathy, since I was unwilling to claim from those 'who called me friend' the sacrifice which I was myself ready to make." That is the confession which many others will share. It can be set down for the sake of others who need not make the same mistake. There are some who are ready to give to them all that they have to give, and it is worth having. Why do without it?

The man within the field of whose life there is not some minister of religion must be unusual. It will seem almost a matter for jest to some readers to say in these days that a minister of the church can help them in their search for God. But why is it thought impossible? It is true that among the thousands who are in this calling some are simply professional, others are officers of an institution, others, though they are probably very few, are insincere. But when this is admitted, there remain in the society in which we live a number of men who early in life had a call to the holy ministry. They might have followed other ways of life; they chose this. For years it was their one concern to prepare themselves for their calling by study and by a life of devotion. They listened to scholars; they read books; they sought to know the Holy Scriptures in the light that modern scholarship could give them. They learned to know the mind of the church, as it can be read in books and in creeds and in sacraments. Afterwards in their own parishes they came to deal with a strangely varied company of men and women and children. If they were true to their calling they were like physicians who have rare opportunities for knowing people. In the medical profession it is recognized that the " local practitioner " has a most important part to play in medical research. I can remember hearing a great specialist give as his testimony that he was dependent upon the detail work of the thousands of general practitioners up and down the land. Was there not a doctor in a tiny village who in a general practice fitted himself to become a leading authority on the heart?

In like manner there are thousands of ministers of religion — general practitioners, if you like — with an experience long and varied and comprehensive who are at your service. Why, for example, let your progress be hindered by false interpretations of the Christian religion which any good minister of the gospel could dispel? As Dr. Edwyn Bevan says:

> What strikes one about most contemporary attacks on Christian views of the world is how seldom they come to close quarters with any Christian view as set forth by its best exponents.

They almost always attack Christianity as they
have found it represented by some poorly educated clergyman in the next street or some dull
traditionalist who taught them at school.*

There is that danger. The way of escape from it
cannot be withdrawal from all helpers, but rather the
seeking out of competent helpers, who are to be found
by those who will look for them. Two examples, out
of many which might easily be given, may serve to
illustrate this truth.

At the music festival in Leeds, England, in 1904,
D. Ffrangçon Davies, a singer whom many still remember with gratitude, was singing the part of Hans
Sachs in *The Mastersingers*. In the audience there
was a man of forty years of age who was seeking help
in his own spiritual life. When he heard the singer,
though the artist was not singing music classed as
sacred, he was deeply stirred and knew that he was
indeed in the presence of a " master singer " and a
master mind and spirit. Two years later this listener
went to see Ffrangçon and, being himself an accomplished amateur singer, arranged to have lessons with
him. In this way he came to understand the quality
and nature of that mysterious something which had
moved him in Leeds. In time that great singer became an informal spiritual director to his student.
How he guided him is told in a little book, *Lead Thou.**
At last in a flash of vision and insight the student
came to see the great sacrifice of Christ and handed
himself over as a living sacrifice to him; and there

* *Christianity* (Thornton Butterworth), p. 253.
* Published by Blackwell.

came joy and peace as in a flood. He hastened to tell Ffrangçon what had happened, and together they sang their doxology. Only once afterward did the student see his master. That was in Liverpool, where Ffrangçon had been singing Elgar's *The Apostles*. In that oratorio there is the incident in which Christ, walking on the waters, says to Peter, " Come." The last words spoken by Ffrangçon as he parted from his friend are recorded: " Now remember, John, Christ has said to you: ' Come.' You have left your boat to come to him. As often as you take your eyes off *him* so often, like Peter, will you sink in the troubled waters of life."

The point of this story is that a helper was at hand for the seeker, and this helper was revealed not in any definitely religious act but in the way in which he was doing his work as a singer. Here was a layman singing a gloriously human part, but singing it in such a way that the spiritual man was revealed.

Though never in the same form, to other seekers the same experience may come if they are ready to accept it when it comes. The sad fact remains that there is help waiting for many a baffled seeker, and either he will not look for it or he is too proud or too shy to take it when it is offered.

The other story is of one known and revered by all who belong to the Student Christian Movement or to the Boys' Brigade, and indeed by all who can remember the closing years of the Victorian era.

The story of Henry Drummond can be told from his side; it can also be told from the side of the thousands of men who sought help from him. For them life would have been different if they had never taken

Drummond into their confidence. One of them said that in after years, when Drummond was dead, he found himself unconsciously praying to him. It was a noble work for that knightly soul to give himself to the students of his day; it was at the same time a right thing for those young men to accept his help in their search for life.

In 1873 Dwight L. Moody and Ira D. Sankey, the two famous American evangelists, went to the British Isles where they were practically unknown. One preached, the other sang the gospel. At first they roused little interest, but when they went north to Newcastle the story of their mission spread to Scotland. Many who were studying for the ministry in that country were drawn into the service of Moody's mission. Among them was Henry Drummond, a student for the ministry, a man whom those who knew him best called a Galahad or a Bayard. Drummond became a teacher of science, a traveler in Central Africa, a speaker to whose quiet and beautiful addresses hearers were eager to listen, whether in his native Scotland or in the west of London or in the growing city of Chicago. But in the school of Moody he learned that the distinctive service which he was to give was to individual souls. They came to know that in this gentle and courteous scholar there was a Greatheart waiting to come to their aid.

If only there were such men everywhere! But perhaps there are more than we are disposed to think. If you would find God it may be that the way appointed for you is to seek some such helper. The way is more open today. There is much more frankness in these days than in the time of our fathers. Then, men might see one another daily, attend the same church, discuss politics and business freely — and never mention the name of God. Today men are much more ready to talk freely upon religion. And in any community there are some at least who are willing to talk seriously and practicably upon the things that concern God and the soul. Why should you not make use of those who desire nothing more than to be used by you?

VII

THE THING THAT CANNOT BE DEFERRED

The night cometh when no man can work.
John 9:4.
The great Enigma is not solved by death but by
life. A *Pilgrim's Quest for the Divine.*

*YOU, but only the Real You, can find God, and that
Real You is a sinner, who needs a Redeemer.*

There are things in our life that can wait and things
that cannot wait. Why does the Christian faith give
urgency to some things and not to others? Why are its
teachers content to leave whole provinces of knowledge unexplored? When they speak of God why
are they content to say of him, "Verily, thou art a
God that hidest thyself"? And in the same breath
with such words they tell us, "Now is the appointed
time." We are encouraged to think of ourselves as
heirs of eternity, and at the same time to remember
that the night cometh when no man can work and
that for such work it is now or never. We have eternity in our heart, and yet we must not waste our life
in time. It is important to get our emphasis right.

Christianity is separated from all religions in which
this earth is treated as a place of unreality and even of
illusion. Rather is it distinguished by the solemn
urgency with which it treats the things that happen in
time. The Christian has never been allowed to sepa-

rate time from eternity, as though, time being short
and fleeting, the things that happen in time can have
no meaning in eternity. For him issues must be determined in time which can be understood only in
the light of eternity. This follows since the Christian
faith is centered not on the Absolute or the Infinite
of which philosophers speak, but on the God who became flesh and dwelt among us. If he has been manifest in the flesh the realm in which life in the flesh
is passed cannot be unreal.

Sometimes Christians have been tempted to take
refuge in the belief that this world of time and space
is to be despised. The first great struggle within the
church was not to keep the belief in the divinity of
Christ, but to hold fast to the reality of his earthly
life. Men hesitated to believe that he could have
been man. But the Christian mind has always clung
to that human life. We can hear the emphatic fall
of the hammer as the words are driven home, " He
was crucified, dead and buried." There was no illusion in the cross. In time the Lord Crucified revealed an eternal reality. Since this is the very heart
of their faith Christians have never been satisfied
with a redemption which was only a play or romance
and would make this life only a trivial prelude to the
real thing — the curtain-raiser before the masterpiece
begins. On the contrary, when they have seriously
thought out their faith they have always believed that
it is theirs in time — it must be historical. We can
escape from many difficulties by abandoning the field
of history, but by escaping in this way we shall lose
our faith altogether. A Christianity made so easy will
cease to exist.

In this life, if this faith is true, there must be urgency, but where is it to be found? What is there in this life of time which is characteristic of it? What is the thing for which we cannot afford to wait? *What happens here?*

If our search for God were for our intellectual satisfaction only there might be reason to suppose that, since God is from eternity the same, the eye of the soul may be able to see him beyond death more clearly than now. So far as intellectual comprehension of God is concerned, we have no access to it now; it must be deferred beyond the bounds of time. Now we see as in a glass darkly; then, and not till then, will we see face to face. We have no reason to think that only in this life must we seek the hidden ways of God. As a philosopher I cannot know all the mysteries of God. But can I, as a sinful man, know him as my Redeemer?

There is a distinction to be made between the understanding of God and the life which is lived by faith in him. In our living we cannot stop the machinery in order that we may think out its mysteries. It is no doubt valuable for a man to understand the science of digestion. But we may study it now or put off the study till a later time, and still go on digesting. We may do the thing without knowing how we do it.

If religion were the scientific explanation of our inward life we might wait till a convenient time came for us to study it. In any case it would be largely a matter for experts. But if the kingdom of God, as we are taught, is not in word, but in power, then clearly we cannot wait for something in it which is all-important.

If indeed we were seeking the evidence for a First Cause, our worship would no doubt be enriched by finding the proof, but we might not discover any change in our practical life; in life we might not be better men, nor braver in death. If we found out this truth only when youth was past we might regret the delay, but we should not think it tragic or irreparable. It is when we come to our religion considered as one of redemption that we begin to understand where the urgency lies.

The only faith with which we have to do is not a creed that teaches us to believe in a First Cause or a Creator or a Supreme Court in the heavens. All this is true. But who could read the New Testament or the liturgies of the church and say that this Christianity is a religion of the First Cause or a worship of the Absolute? The cry that is heard and answered is not, " Who will give me light? " but, " What must I do to be saved? " It brings the offer from the God of holy love, not of a life enlightened or even reformed, but delivered and made new. The Lord Christ is said to have brought into human life a revolution: " Old things are passed away: behold they are become new." Since therefore we are dealing with such a newly released power which does things, then it makes a difference *when* it is released and when things are done. If, for example, youth becomes one thing in the faith of Christ and another and an entirely different thing with Christ, then something is lost when youth does not find Christ — something that cannot be gained equally well in manhood or age.

If it is no exaggeration but a plain statement of fact that St. Paul lived, and yet not he but Christ in

him, then it was a matter of importance to him —
and he knew it — that for years before the light came
to him he had missed it.

This is not to be considered by the customary measures of gain and loss. We do not think rightly as
long as we move in the realm of prudence or security
or as though we had to make provision against a
possible doom after death. If it were a question for
us of taking out a policy of security then a change at
the last moment might be enough. If I am taking
out a life policy and finish the negotiations in good
time, however near to the end, the policy stands. I
shall have lost only whatever relief of mind I might
have had during the earlier years, but nothing more.

We cannot deal with God on any footing of this
kind. It is a serious danger that we are likely to think
of him by analogies taken from human life not at its
best, but from its meaner ways. Man has brought
often to the interpretation of his religion not his best,
but his worst qualities. The truth has to be faced,
as it was once said, that man may cling to God with
his weakness and find in his God a larger self — himself cast upon the screen of the universe, himself
arbitrary, acquisitive, revengeful, even deceitful. If
God were such, and the only matter of importance
were to be in his favor, then it would not matter greatly
whether the necessary steps were taken today or to-
morrow. It might even be doubtful whether they
should be taken at all.

But with the God whose face we have seen in
Jesus Christ all merely formal submission counts for
nothing. All analogies from insurance against loss
are idle. No less are the analogies from tyrannies. It

was not to enlist slaves to do his bidding blindly that God made this creation; it was that his children might be trained *in time* to become his sons, and sons who enter in some measure into his holy love. That must be the reason why in time certain things cannot be postponed, why there are works to be done before this day ends, and only then; since the night cometh when no man can work. Such works must have to do with the distinctive character of this life, and that distinctive character lies in moral obedience.

When we have come so far we are faced by one fact difficult to many modern readers and yet transparently clear in the New Testament — the one urgent, central, all-determining fact that God is related to man not first of all as the Almighty to his creature, nor as the mysterious Cause of all things to the thinker, but to all men wise or simple as the Saviour to the saved. It is with sin we have to deal in this earthly life; if we are to find God, we cannot defer to some future day our facing this fact of sin and of forgiveness.

" Seek ye the Lord while he may be found. Call ye upon him while he is near: let the wicked forsake his way, and the unrighteous man his thoughts, and let him return unto the Lord and he will have mercy upon him."

If it is in moral obedience that the secret lies, then the tragedy of sin must be faced. We must listen to the call for repentance.

What the prophet had demanded the Lord himself also demanded. Jesus came into Galilee preaching good news of God and declaring that the kingdom of God was at hand, and saying, " Repent ye." Those

who took up his word — St. Paul and all the apostles
— call with one voice upon men everywhere to repent.
If we are thinking of the search for God we come to
this serious call from which we cannot escape.

There are gods of another character whom we may
think we find. But if God is what the Christian faith
believes him to be, the holy Father, then to seek for
him is vain unless we are ready to deal with the last
fact of all. We shall not find him except as sinners
find their Saviour. We shall not enter into his kingdom except as those who have been redeemed. Other
things can wait; this cannot. The character of all the
days of our life is determined by this relationship.
Our lives will come to their full fruitage and bear their
divine harvest to the degree that we face these two
most tremendous facts: we are sinful men; and God
is in Christ reconciling us to himself, and to himself
as the holy Lord.

We can have confirmation of this truth in the story
of those who have been this way before us. If we
ask where these others have found God, we shall find
ourselves in a world with a language unfamiliar to our
ears. We shall need to learn that language. Sin,
judgment, forgiveness, holiness have become to us
technical words to be studied in the light of history,
but without relation to our policy of life. Everyone
who preaches today knows that he speaks to hearers
with whom he cannot begin where preachers could
once begin.

" What in the dickens is sin? " a student inquired
of a professor of biblical literature. The student is
not alone. What *is* sin? That is a question prior to
many others. What is repentance; forgiveness; the

new birth; the life of sanctity? It is of little use to take any of these words for granted. To tell some hearers today that they must repent is to speak in a foreign tongue. To introduce them to a world in which this is a cardinal necessity is to leave them perplexed and bewildered. They are willing to let words stand in the ritual of the church; they belong to a tradition which they do not wish to banish. But what it means for them to repent they do not know.

If God is set before them as the eternal Truth, they can understand how he may answer the cry of their souls, " Give me reality."

If he is set before them as Beauty, so old and yet so new, they will know him as the answer to their cry: " Give me the vision of that beauty which I have loved, though so late. Let the beauty of the Lord our God be upon me."

But there is another cry which was once the most bitter cry of all: " Give me holiness; set me free from sin." But is that a cry which means to us what it meant to the psalmists or to the apostles? This question must be borne in mind even while at all costs we keep from unreal words. If " sin " and " repentance " are no longer words with their old meaning we must not pretend that they are. The men of olden times spoke of the burden of sin as intolerable; is it intolerable to us? They wrote such words as those of the fifty-first Psalm: " Have mercy upon me, O God, according to thy lovingkindness "; or the seventh chapter of Romans: " Who shall deliver me from the body of this death? " But is it a body of death to us?

But we should not assume that we are right in dismissing the language of that lost world as old and outworn. What we are concerned with is not a mere dialect invented and used by the church. We shall find vast areas of our human inheritance lost to us if we cease to know the meaning of sin and judgment. The thought that man is a sinner is not only in the very texture of the Christian religion; it is essential to all the greatest literature. If we do not find any meaning in sin we shall fail to understand not only Dante, but also Shakespeare. Who can read *Lear* or *Othello* without keeping in mind the mystery of sin? Where lies the one eternal theme of tragedy but in the human will, tempted, torn, resisting, yielding, remorseful, despairing, doomed to judgment? Leave out the conception of conscience, and what becomes of tragedy, whether it is the Greek tragedies or the Elizabethan, or the plays of Ibsen? If a modern man is unwilling to read the Epistle to the Romans he can read *Crime and Punishment* or *Peer Gynt* and he will still ask, " What is sin? "

But it may be held that, serious as the loss of the great tragedies would be, we might *have* to do without them, and the time must come in which *Othello* will be as remote from our culture as the fifty-first Psalm or the seventh chapter of Romans. That may come to pass. But we must not cast away the universal tradition of the human spirit without knowing what we are doing. We must at least face the seriousness of the change, which must be nothing less than a revolution in the inner life of man. Before we accept it as a loss, necessary though to be regretted, we might well ask how far we *have* outlived, not the language, but the spiritual experiences which found expression in it.

We must prepare ourselves for the call to repentance for sin not by any journeys to far-off lands but by looking at the world from the place where we stand.

How can we explain what is wrong with the world? Or rather why do we say that something is wrong with the world? What standard have we by means of which we can say that life falls short? I must ask this question; but why must I ask it? So far as we can tell the human family alone of all the creatures of the earth asks such questions. Man alone inquires, "What is wrong with the world?" Man alone has a picture before his mind of what the earth *might be like*. He alone measures it by a standard of hidden values.

But what *is* wrong? It is certainly not the lack of knowledge only, though we have no right to think of knowledge as if it makes no difference. We must have knowledge, whatever else we have; but it is not a complete answer to say that if we only knew enough the wrong in the world would disappear.

The difference between man as he is today and as he might be in a changed world must be measured not only in terms of knowledge but also in terms of will, and of will at the service of love. We must desire different things, we must be ready to do different things, if we are to be set free. To that answer we move by the sheer pressure of facts.

It is a common experience for anyone who lives near a great city to look over the valley to the hills on the other side. From there the city, vast in its population, looks like a monstrous village. There is something wonderful and exhilarating in the sight of a city. Within it are many brave and patient workmen of God, servants of whom he is not ashamed. Within it are artists, craftsmen, poets, musicians, scholars spending their days in search of truth, lovers of their fellows fighting for justice. There no appeal to the heart of man will miss its response. There saints are offering up their prayers and martyrs are dying. On the altars of ten thousand homes the fire of pure love is kept burning.

But what is wrong there? What is it that turns into evil the instinct by virtue of which the noblest achievements of man are wrought? Why does the instinct of adventure which leads men to take the hazards of the explorer become degraded to the ugly and selfish passion of the gambler? Why is love degraded to lust? What is wrong?

If we answer that question we shall know more of the God whom we must seek in that city. He must be One who deals with that very thing that is wrong. He must be One who can deal with that wrong now. There can be no answer to this need of ours in some other world or beyond the limits of time. We must have a God who can come to our rescue now.

You can find such a God there in the city. But you must be ready to find him in judgment and in mercy — in judgment, for only in judgment can he reveal his mercy, and in judgment which begins not with *them* but with *you*.

The reality and the horror of sin can still be brought home to those who are prepared to look at the world with honest eyes. Those who doubt might read, or reread, the story of Josephine Butler. This woman left with all who knew her such memories as saints leave. She belonged to the company of St. Catherine and St. Theresa, of Elizabeth Fry and Sister Dora —

saints with the power to translate their visions into action. In her home she heard the cry of the women of England who had been wronged by the passing of the Contagious Diseases Act. These women were what is called " lost," but for her they were sisters for whom Christ died, not chattels for the use of men. The story of the battle that she and her friends fought and won is one of the noblest in the history of Christ and his people. In that story anyone who chooses can read the secret of sin.

One of these poor girls for whom she cared, near the end of her life said to Josephine Butler: " When your soul quails at the sight of the evil, which will increase yet awhile, dear Mrs. Butler, think of me and take courage. God has given me to you that you may never despair of any."

Of another there is this record:

> She drew us near to her by the appeal of her earnest eyes, and raising her right hand high, with a strangely solemn gesture, and with a look full of heroic and desperate resolve, she said: " I will fight for my soul through hosts and hosts and hosts. . . ." " Poor brave child," I cried to her, " you will find on the other shore One waiting for you who has fought through all those hosts for you, who will not treat you as man has treated you." *

It was in dealing not with statistics and acts of Parliament only but with living souls that the fire was kept burning with such a fierce and steady glow through the years of that long campaign. The nature of the

* Josephine Butler, *Life of George Butler* (Arrowsmith).

injustice against which Josephine Butler fought was kept steadily before her in flesh and blood. It was no abstract evil against which she fought. What is wrong in the world is to be sought not in abstractions but in persons.

If we want to know what sin means it can be learned here. If we are tempted to explain away the evil that is in the world by a hasty and superficial use of psychology we shall learn our error; we shall be " convicted of sin," as our fathers used to say. And once more we shall be carried to the house of Simon the leper and hear the comforting words of the Saviour: " Her sins which are many are forgiven her because she loved much."

But it is one mark of our modern attitude toward life that we are quick to see ourselves as bound up with the social and international order. If " sin " is to mean much to us it will have to be interpreted for us in all the relationships of our life.

Dickens in *Hard Times* drew the character of Mr. Gradgrind, a hard, merciless manufacturer in the days when, in order to amass wealth rapidly, men found comfort in the separation of their business practices, which were under " economic law," from their religion. If Mr. Gradgrind had been called a sinner he might have answered with anger: " What do you mean? I am sober; I pay my debts; I am not an adulterer or a thief; I tell the truth "; and such an answer might have been satisfactory at one time to many companies of Christian people. It is not satisfactory today. We should reply, " All these commandments you may have kept, but you are not therefore free from sin. You have treated human beings as tools to minister to your greed. You have missed the presence of Christ in them; he is hungry and you have not fed him, sick and you have not cared for him. You have set up a screen that you call ‘ economic necessity ’ to conceal your real motives of selfishness and greed. If the will of the Most High is the same today as it was when Isaiah prophesied and the apostles witnessed to Christ, then you are a sinner in need of forgiveness and mercy.”

There is no reason why we should treat sin as a word descriptive only of the individual life; it can be used and must be used in our discussion of social and national choices. There is guilt upon the soul of a people; and it is to a nation, as to an individual soul, that the words of the prophet still come. To that also we must come if we would deal with sin in a realistic way.

But we shall not escape from the call to penitence by putting all the blame for what is wrong upon the community. We shall not plead that there is no necessity for us personally to stand before the judgment seat of Christ on the excuse that it was not we but the church or the nation which was to blame. If we are to find the God who is revealed in Jesus Christ our Lord, and find him in all his grace and power, we must expose ourselves to his searching light. We shall confess: “ I am the social problem. I am the problem of war. I am the man who must know God’s judgment and receive his mercy.”

This chapter has been long and discursive. Questions have been asked and the shaping of the answers has been left to the reader. But an attempt must be made to gather up some of the threads.

We live in a world in which something is wrong. There is in human life a false principle at work. It has its hold upon the will of man. It makes him do the thing that he would not. It turns human society, which should be a scene of cooperation, into one of war. It makes the loveliest things on earth shameful things from which men turn their faces. It changes love into lust, adventure into gambling, fellowship into a selfish policy of each for himself.

The very hold upon us of this false principle which we call sin makes it necessary for us to seek deliverance. We know how idle it is to give good advice, or to receive it, if nothing more is available; we need a hand not our own to lift us now above what we can be unaided.

Sin is a disease of the will. We must have a physician. What is wrong with us is not ignorance nor folly, but this disease which holds us down where we are most ourselves. Jesus said the will is in the control of " the Prince of this world."

This disease has not only made us do things which were false to our true life, but it has made us into personalities with this sad distinction, that we alone of the creatures of earth betray our own life. We sin against God.

When we speak of forgiveness we mean that miracle whereby, in place of bondage to this evil principle, we are given a new freedom. In place of a broken relationship there is a new restored relationship of the child to his Father. We are at peace with God. And when to this we add, " through our Lord Jesus Christ," we make clear to ourselves why it was that Jesus Christ came, suffered, died and rose again. It was not to enlighten us only or to give us good counsel, but to deliver us from the power which holds us down and to restore us to the true relationship to God. It was this strange and wonderful thing which he did for us. He came to bring us to God.

Repentance is the adjustment of all our being to this new fact. It means the turning away from the old life of sin. But in the New Testament it is more often considered as the turning *to* something. The repentant soul looks away to the Lord in whom the kingdom has drawn near. Faith must be the act of surrender to that Lord in all the range of his truth and grace. " *I believe, I belong.*"

All these things we must prove in our own experiences. The serious matter is that they must be proved in experience *now*. Other things may wait. These cannot.

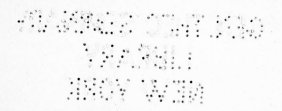

VIII

THE SEEKER WHO IS SOUGHT

YOU cannot find God without seeking; but will all your seeking find him unless something else can be said concerning him? *Can man by searching find out God?* There can be only one possible answer if all the searching is on the side of man. If God can be perfectly described as the God who hides himself then the human seeker is playing a tragic game of hide-and-seek; he cannot hope to do more than touch the outermost reaches of the kingdom; he will seek and never find.

We are driven to reconsider the seeking of man, still in the light of what we believe man to be.

What are the choices among which we must decide when we try to answer this question? There may be before man at least three possible ways of making sense of his life. He may be explained as a seeker, or as one who is sought, or as both seeker and sought.

He is a seeker. Of that we have no doubt. In every field of his life, from the beginning, his characteristic role has been that of the explorer and the pilgrim. All his earthly pilgrimages are a sign that his life itself is a pilgrimage in eternity.

But many, with the same facts before them, can explain the many movements of man's heart and mind only by the truth that man is entirely in the hands of his God. When God needs man he seeks him and will not let him go. If he does not need man, then man is left alone. Man cannot of himself find God. All is of God.

Others there are who cannot be satisfied that either explanation makes sense of the experiences which man has put on record. They do not pretend to have found any complete and final system in which man will know as he is known, nor can they be content with a compromise. Taking away part of the claim for man as a seeker and part of the claim for him as one sought, they invite him to think of himself as a neutral figure somewhere between the two — a tamer, reduced being, not in reality all that we mean by a seeker nor all that we should expect of one who is sought. But this will not do; whatever else man is he is not a poor half-and-half creature. If he were, how does it happen that he harbors such wild hopes and such dark despair? Why has he never been content with a safe and satisfactory midway position?

There is one more explanation. We may refuse to accept the dilemma " either . . . or " and say boldly, " *Man is both* " — both seeker and sought. The time is not yet ripe for our understanding of how that can be. At present we have only some facts before us, and those we have are fragmentary and unarranged and easily misread. It is always necessary to guard against a hasty attempt to present a complete account of human life.

It is best to accept the mystery in this strange matter in which we have no parallel to guide us. Human life is a thing by itself; we may understand many of its phases while all the time we know that we are dealing with a mystery. We shall learn all that life means when the shadows flee away, but not now. Our present wisdom is to hold firmly to that which we know and to refuse to construct prematurely complete systems.

It may well be asked: If there are various ways of explaining the same facts, to what authority should we listen? Who has the best right to speak? Has one man any more right than another to say whether the human facts are best explained by the belief that man seeks, or that he is sought, or that he is himself both the seeker and the sought?

For the evidence we must go to the inner life of man, for who else can speak for man save he himself? We have to do with the spirit of man as that has been revealed. It is impossible, for example, to form any judgment of poetry without the evidence of the poets. Others may " reason and welcome," but only these can know. In like manner, the saints' evidence of their own inner life can be given only by them. The evidence for the experience of Christ which made life new for St. Paul could have been neither produced nor explained by the men who sat in judgment upon him — by Felix or Festus or Agrippa or Nero. It might be true or not; these men could only say, " We do not know."

But if the evidence of that for which we seek explanation comes from such men — prophets, or poets, or saints — there is some reason for asking as well their explanation of their experience. They may very well say not only, " This happened to me," but " When it happened it clearly came from a certain source of which

I can testify." If they give us an explanation there
must be something within us that confirms it. In the
language which an old friend loved to use, " They ring
the bell within us." But we shall be foolish if we wait
till we have risen to the experience of the saints before
we accept their faith. Our Lord said, " He that re-
ceiveth a prophet in the name of a prophet shall receive a prophet's reward," and this reward may be the
joyful assurance that the word which has come to the
prophet is the word of the living God. We may receive a prophet and in our own measure enter into his
vision.

There is no one who can speak upon the character
and source of the experience of man in his dealings
with God with such authority as those for whom these
things are not hearsay, but first-hand realities.

For what, then, must we go to our authorities?

If it were true that man seeks, and that nothing
more is known of him but that, we should expect him
to show a certain character. His make-up would present little mystery. We do know him as seeker, but
we are left with much in his own account of himself
which will not fit into this theory at all. Certainly he
is always seeking — but he has never believed that this
urge to seek explains his life. He has gained something, but he can never say that he has won it by himself; he cannot escape from the suspicion that it may
have been given to him. He has an inner life of his
own about which he knows little; but what he does
know shows it to be an arena in which many powers are
at work. Who or what these powers are he can only
conjecture, but he knows enough to be certain that he
is not to be explained as a self-contained, self-directed

being. Whatever else he may be, he is not a self-made man.

Man's very seekings are not easy to explain. He can understand, indeed, why he must go out as a huntsman seeking for food and clothing. But why is he prepared to fling away life itself for some gain which by the standard of utility is worth nothing or less than nothing? Why should he leave his home and cross the margin of that world which lies beyond the horizon? Why should he watch through the night reading the stars? It seems to him at least reasonable to conjecture that in these promptings Someone or Something is moving him. Man has always had, and still has, suspicion that he is the quarry of some Power which seeks him. It is not conceit that leads him to think that he is of some importance in the universe of which he is a part; it is reasonable inference from the facts, as he has understood them, of his own life.

Man must be true to facts. To reach a logical conclusion by omitting one or other of them, or by shaping them, taking off a little here and a little there, is unthinkable to a man who takes life seriously. No explanation is worth anything which does not cover the crude and formless facts. Better no explanation at all than a juggled answer! Meanwhile there are clues, hints, surmises which have been provided for us by our most credible witnesses; to them man must give attention. He cannot delight, as the writer of fiction may, in weaving mysteries with the purpose of explaining them at the end. Whatever else human life may be it is not a mystery story designed by the divine Artist to keep us guessing till the end.

Seeker or sought or both. If we suppose that life is

a drama, it is not one in which the players need count themselves helpless or paralyzed till the final curtain falls and they discover the plot in all its unwindings: they can know enough for the moment, enough to move *with* the main action. The final mystery in which all the discords will be resolved and all the tragic happenings be seen as part of the divine comedy can be left.

It is at least man's part to declare that, being what he is so far as he now can know the facts, he is not the sole master of his own thought and action. If he were of such character he knows that he would not feel as he does feel or think as he does think.

But again: if, impressed by the thought of this Other who lays his hand upon him, man puts aside all belief in his own freedom, he may come to think of himself as an automaton. There are ingenious craftsmen who can make marionettes act as though they were intelligent human beings, so cleverly do they pull the strings. Man has often played with the thought that he is himself a marionette pulled by celestial strings. He is nothing; God is all. God pulls his creatures here and there; of one he makes a king, of another a beggar, according to the demands of his plot. When the play is over the dolls are packed away in their box. They have known nothing about the play. They share neither in the tragedy nor in the comedy.

But if man were this kind of creature would he be as he is today? If St. Francis had been a marionette, would he have been St. Francis as we know him? In one of his books Maurois pictures a moment when the marionettes begin to know the character of the plot in which they are playing; that is the end of their part as marionettes. That is precisely the position of man in the drama. He thinks, and he cannot help thinking what the drama means. Why? The moment the marionette begins to know that he is a marionette, he ceases to be one. If man were but a creature pulled by strings he would cease to be man. He would not be moved by the agonies or raptures which have visited him. The saints at least are clear about this. No less clear are the poets and prophets.

No one who saw the play *R.U.R.* or heard it on the radio will forget the plot which has given the new word "robot" to our language. Certain scientists made creatures who were able to do all the manual labor of the world; they were almost perfect machines. What caused the disaster which made these creatures masters of the world? One of the scientists by a clever experiment gave to them the sense of pain; they began to have an emotional life, and this at once made them cease to be machines. It is impossible for man, who suffers, to count himself only a marionette or a robot. If he were that he would not know pain or joy; but he does know pain and joy. If he were that he would not be troubled about the plot; but he does trouble about it. "Oh that I knew where I might find him! That I might come even to his seat."

For the moment an appeal must be made to the facts as they are presented to us. We cannot give a final verdict. But there is at least reason for leaving open the possibility that we are neither self-directed nor pulled by strings. It is conceivable that while we seek and must seek with as much energy and courage and patience as if everything depended upon us, at the same time an "unweariable Adventurer" is seeking for our souls.

The evidence of the saints is important, and they speak for each man. They can speak where he is dumb. They have advanced further, but they are on the same road. A man may talk of himself as being a plain unemotional, practical, unspiritual individual. He may even explain away such religion as he once had; that looks to him now like the afterglow of a sun which has set not to rise again. But all the time the saints are there with their confident bearing, giving the lie to him.

Nothing is more difficult than to discover what the ordinary man thinks about his own inner life, but it is wise to disregard his merely superficial account of himself. Very often his words are a smoke screen, deliberately set up to hide his real mind. Even such words as he uses confirm the suspicion that he has never escaped from the sense of the mystery of his own life. He may call his former beliefs only the by-products of adolescence, but when he is far removed from the realm of argument he cannot deny that those experiences had at least the signs of reality. It is possible for a man to doubt in words the reality of all his inner life, the reality of its doubts and denials no less than of its faith. But he does not deceive us and he does not deceive himself; if there is any reality anywhere it was known to him that night when the pleading of an inspired voice awakened echoes in that innermost region in which man knows that he is most himself.

There is a passage in *Saul* in which Browning de-

scribes such a man in such an hour of spiritual awaken-
ing.   David had found in his love for Saul the King
a clue to the love of God for man:

" I know not too well how I found my way home in the
      night.
   There were witnesses, cohorts about me, to left and
      to right,
   Angels, powers, the unuttered, unseen, the alive, the
      aware:
   I repressed, I got through them as hardly, as strug-
      glingly there,
   As a runner beset by the populace famished for
      news —
   Life or death.   The whole earth was awakened, hell
      loosed with her crews;
   And the stars of night beat with emotion, and tingled
      and shot
   Out in fire the strong pain of pent knowledge: but I
      fainted not,
   For the Hand still impelled me at once and sup-
      ported, suppressed
   All the tumult, and quenched it with quiet and holy
      behest,
   Till the rapture was shut in itself, and the earth
      sank to rest."

   That is poetry, and therefore some readers will view
it with suspicion.   But because it is poetry, it is therefore the truth about ourselves.   Let it be read as a
record of that exaltation which comes at one time
or other to every man.   Is it right to call it unreal
although a thousand other experiences have made us
forget it or be false to it?

When St. Augustine — to quote him once more — recalled his own youth he said, " But was it life, O my God? " When we go over our memories of the past, where do we discover that which we can best call life?

It is always possible and sometimes easy to explain these inner experiences as if they could be accounted for by the physical conditions under which they occurred, and without doubt the physical has its place in the explanation. But when we have studied these causes and allowed for them, we are still left in mystery. Let us illustrate.

If a mouse lived within the case of a piano he might see the hammers fall and, after certain movements of these hammers, might perceive certain sounds to follow. If he were a speculative mouse he might seek the explanation of the sounds. It might even be contended by one mouse that these hammers gave a complete explanation of the sounds; and he would not be wrong. But on the other side there is the player whose striking the keys makes the hammers move and the music sound. It is perfectly true that the fall of the hammer goes with the sound, but that alone does not account for the sound; if the sounds were without relation to one another they might be explained by the movement of a dog over the keyboard. But if there were any ordered grouping of the sounds it would not be possible to explain them by the mechanical movements which could be seen. If the hammers were playing a prelude of Bach it would not be possible to explain the sounds by the casual pressure of keys. Some player must be there who has learned the master's work, and behind him we see the master himself, living still in the work upon which he impressed his mind. We hear the sounds; we know the mechanical causes; but there is a master who makes the music.

This is only an imperfect illustration, as all illustrations in this field must be; but at least it suggests how we may miss the real explanation of those thoughts and aspirations which visit us in our inner life. They can be explained by the immediate conditions — our range of vision, the things which we have seen and heard, even the state of our health — but all the time there is Another, hidden from us, whose hand alone can supply the secret of our life, whose voice alone can give the reason for those echoes which reverberate in the soul. That knocking which we hear will not be explained till the door is opened and the Lord himself is seen standing there. "Behold he stands at the door and knocks."

By this it is not meant that we should blindly decide to accept the explanation that our experiences are what they are because of the divine hand's pressure upon us. But there is at least good reason for saying that the door is not closed to the belief that we have other entrances into the soul than those which we can explain as originating in ourselves. We can at least say that there is a case to be heard. Witnesses can be called to tell us whether or not, in their own judgment, they were what they were because of the approach to them of a divine Seeker.

Three witnesses may be called. First is the prophet. What is true of one is true of all the prophets; they confess with one voice that they were called and chosen by a heavenly Power. God speaks and they answer. "The Lord God hath spoken, who can but prophesy?"

So Amos cried in the wilderness of Tekoa. And in the
opening of the book of Isaiah we read the story of a
call which prompted that noble statesman and prophet
through the long years of his life: " In the year that
King Uzziah died I saw also the Lord high and lifted
up, and his train filled the temple. . . . Also I heard
the voice of the Lord God saying unto me. . . ."

Isaiah was sought. Of that he was sure as he was
of nothing else. " Dreamer! Visionary! " we cry. But
there was no man in Jerusalem who could read as he
read the signs of his times, no man who was more
fearless a realist. He became a statesman before whom
kings trembled in their intrigues, in whose presence
the little and cunning politicians of Jerusalem seemed
blind cowards. Through a long life he was sustained
by that vision which was given to him. He was always
a man who had been called and commissioned; the
voice had come to him first of all and he had answered;
God spoke first.

The poets bear witness to the same truth. In the
moments in which they were most themselves they
were held by the hands of Another. They say as the
psalmist said:

> " Nevertheless I am continually with thee.
>   Thou has holden me by my right hand,
>   Thou shalt guide me with thy counsel
>   And afterwards receive me to glory."

There are other voices calling man. They may lead
him to his own undoing. There are sirens seeking
to entice him as they enticed Ulysses and his men.
Still there are voices calling the unsatisfied heart of
man. Titan as he is, star-measurer, he " makes, but

half-aware of what he makes." Man is striving with himself,

" He burns with the old need onward still to strain,
  Mis-timed, way-lost, defaulting."*

And for him there waits the undiscovered country.
The end of his adventures has not come. There are
still wonders and glories to be sought, and still out of
the silence and the unknown there is One who seeks
and draws his spirit and will not leave him.

Here is man, his heart so hardly taught. Of him
eternity has need. For him a Lover, an unweariable
Adventurer makes his quest. And now he can face all
the storms that beat upon him. He will not fail in the
end, whatever comes.

" He that has so loved peril in all experience,
  He that has followed sorrow all her way,
  Will not now refuse or shrink; prove him to the
      uttermost,
  With worse than worst confront him! "

In such an hour he will stand forth greater in his naked-
ness, for there are " powers from far that replenish
him," and this is his security. He is not alone and
can never be forsaken. And with this faith he can
move into the undiscovered world.

" Dawning beyond knowledge, vision shall deliver him
  From all that flattered, threatened, soiled, betrayed.
  Lo, having nothing, he is free of all the universe,
  And where light is, he enters unafraid."

   * No nobler poem has been written on this subject than " The
Sirens" by Laurence Binyon. (*Collected Poems*, Macmillan.)

This is the ancient and undying belief of man, that there is Someone seeking him. The mystics have never doubted it. They have known that the one way to fly from God is to fly to him.

> "When we could not fly from Thee anywhere
> We fled to Thee."

They have told of the Hound of Heaven. They have likened life to a game of hide-and-seek in which it appears sometimes as though man were hiding from his God who seeks him, and at other times as though man were seeking and God were hiding his face.

But it may well be that the poet speaks most surely to our condition when he tells us, with all the wealth of his imagination, that we belong indeed to a race that seeks, but that this is not the last word: we belong to a race that is sought. Upon this we rest our hope. Through all things in the heavens and in the earth moves that mighty Lover in quest of us. And we can move onward, sure that man is not the victim of any delusion or wild surmise when he obeys the voices.

It is not for the poet to turn his theme into the language of religion. But others may seek to trace what in the Christian faith it is that corresponds to the poet's belief that man is the seeker who is sought. Certainly this conviction lies at the very heart of Christian truth. In the language of theology it is the doctrine of grace. It is the very secret of the incarnation — that God sought man and gave his Son. We love because God first loved us. No one can read the New Testament without finding everywhere this daring, "heart-shattering" belief.

Sometimes in the religious life the stress is laid upon the seeking of man. There have been and still are teachers who will put all the emphasis upon the quest from the human side. There are others who begin with the quest of God. For them man is a being dearly loved and sought. They think of him as redeemed and called into the divine life. All around him and surging within him are the mighty powers of grace, of divine love in action. Man is both — seeker and sought. But he is first of all — the sought.

To seek, if that were all, would be a hard and unprofitable task. What chance of finding would there be! To be sought, if that were all, would be an experience but little worth. The Christian truth is that man is sought, but that he also must seek, earnestly and diligently, as if all depended upon him. But first comes the assurance from our Lord and his apostles that man is sought; not that he loves, but he is loved. Then the seeking and the adventure follow.

There is more than a technical difference here. Much of our religious life is fitful and ineffective because there is wanting at the heart of it the assurance that we are not left to ourselves, nor are we friendless in the eternal world. For there is comfort and patience and hope in the knowledge that our redemption and our eternal life are not our concern alone.

Christian hearts, indeed, will declare that they know who is that unweariable Adventurer who makes his quest of them. There is only one better experience than to be sought; it is to be found. And if we are seeking and he is seeking, the finding must follow soon or late.

IX

WAYS IN WHICH HE MAY FIND US

Where was thy body, so broken for me,
    Lord, my Lord?
When didst thou shed thy blood for me,
    Jesus, Lord?
Has it never been broken on any tree,
Since they lifted thee down from Calvary?
Have thy wounds been stanched since Calvary,
    Lord, my Lord?

" Here is my body, still broken for thee,
    Soul, my soul;
Now I am shedding my blood for thee,
    Soul for soul;
While they grind the corn in the mill for me,
While they tread the grapes for a sign of me,
I am broken and bleeding for love of thee,
    Soul, my soul."

IF IT were said to someone seeking for God that
he should seek him in church he might lift his eye-
brows with surprise. In church! What is there to
be found in church?

Earlier in this book the church has been considered
from the side of the human seeker. But it may be
also considered as a way in which the Lord is waiting
to meet with us. It has a place in our lives; has it a
place also in his?

We shall be wise to visit and indeed to haunt the

places in which God is to be found. Even if we can say no more than that he has been reported in those places, we shall not neglect them.

The church is called the Church of Christ; it is at the same time a society of human beings, bearing the marks of human folly and ignorance and sin. Can the two things be said of the same society? Where if anywhere are we to look for the body of Christ in which he can still be found?

It is indeed in living men and women if anywhere that we must look for the continuous life of the church of Christ. It is not to any *invisible* church that we must look. What use is it to tell us while we are in this world of time and space that we may find God in some ideal society which has no relation to the society in which we spend our days?

If we are told that we may find Christ in the church we take that to mean in the church as it is known to us today, not in any invisible society. We must understand by it individual churches, not first of all " Mount Zion and the innumerable company of angels and the church of the firstborn who are in heaven." That also is ours in promise but it cannot give us what we need now and here. Here the difficulty arises. Can we expect that God will seek for us in these societies as we know them?

We may think for encouragement of the problem that faced St. Paul when, for example, he lived, as he did for some time, in Corinth. He was walking, let us say, one first day of the week to the meeting place of the first disciples in Corinth when he met a rabbi of friendly disposition with whom he stopped to talk.

" What do you expect to find when you meet with your new friends? " the rabbi asked. " Are they all men and women of holy character in whose faces the eternal Light shines? "

" Not in the least," St. Paul answered. " They are of all kinds. They are weighed down by their past sins. They are sensual, self-willed, quarrelsome, even vicious. But how am I different from them? And there is another side. In their lives I see a new life beginning. It is as though I stand at the dawn of a new day. In that upper room I expect to find the first-born of a new world."

" What do you mean by finding Christ there? "

" Christ for me is not one man to be separated from all who belong to him. Where he is there are his members. Where his members are there he is. And these are his members. What they are now anyone can see. What they are to be only the eye of God can see. But we have prophecies and promises and in them we can see God. You see why I am going to meet with God."

Is that experience outside our range today? Is it enough to say, as many do, that the church is unworthy of its name and they are wiser who seek other ways into the secret of the universe?

There was a well known writer who explained in his youth that he did not go to church because he did not want to set a bad example. And if we set ourselves above others and despised them we might agree that to go to church with them was no way for us. We shall certainly find in church a company at one in this: that they are weak and tempted and sinful. But who are we to separate ourselves from them? Some of our dislike for them may be due to taste; like others, we mistake refinement for holiness. But, as the apostle said, we are " one in Adam." The fact that we shall pass the hour of worship with others who are very much like ourselves is no reason for staying away from church, nor does it provide a ground for the suspicion that we shall not find God waiting there and God there in those very imperfect human beings.

We may begin with the people assembled. We take our place among them. They and we are dealing in a greater or less degree with the same mysterious realities. Our personalities, like sensitive plates, are exposed to the same vision. We are assembled to listen to the same voice. And there is some response, however little, in every hearer. And in those responses we find God.

I heard of a man who had no taste for classical music, and when one day for some reason he went to a concert, he sat there hoping that the time would pass quickly. Suddenly he looked at the face of a man to whom the glory of that music was revealed. In his eyes he saw a light which he had not known before. So it may happen that in the face of someone near you in church you may see a light not yet known to you. That one does not know of the light (the less he knows of it the better), but you do.

Can we forget that mysterious reality which the New Testament calls the communion of the Holy Spirit? This is one way in which we can experience it. Communion means having and enjoying something in common. It is not as though we had come to a common meal to which each of us, as at a picnic, had brought his own portion. The communion of the

Holy Spirit does not mean that a number of men and women come together to pool all their good thoughts and desires. It is not a meeting of a cooperative society. On the contrary, it is a sharing together in the thing which is given by the one Lord and distributed to each man as he has need and as he has capacity to understand and to receive the gift. So when we go to church we do not go to do the other people good by any excellence of our own. We are going to learn what can be learned by the members of a company all of whom, varied as they are, have exposed their spirit to the one word and the one action of the living God.

He draws near; he speaks; he acts. But the word of this living God is not understood till it is answered. The answer belongs to the word itself. The word is not spoken into the air. The word of God does not return empty, but it accomplishes the thing to do which it is sent; and until it accomplishes this the word is not perfectly fulfilled. What that word in Christ accomplishes is seen in the eyes of those who are listening. Still more will it be seen in their lives. To be with them is to be in the presence not only of the word, but of the answer to the word; and there also is Almighty God.

The very building, to one who uses his imagination, is rich in the memory of others who in that same place once sought and found God. There can be no such thing as an empty church. The ancient cathedrals are filled with the generations of the faithful dead. If we go to Assisi we do not count it deserted or solitary. St. Francis is there still to the inward eye. In the church to which we go we can find the silence filled

with other voices. We can know how God was once
with them and how they made their answer, though in
other language and oppressed by other burdens than
those which we carry. They live still because of all
that they received from their God, and being in him
they can never die. Through them he still comes to us.

He meets us in his Word.

That God speaks to us in his Word is the faith of
all Christian people, but if they are invited to explain
how he speaks they do not agree. Sometimes they
make a sharp distinction between the human element
and the divine. They call upon us to decide on which
side we are to take our stand. They say that the
Bible is *either* human *or* divine. But why should we
accept this " either . . . or "?

Such a word must indeed be human: what other
language could be used in speaking to men? There
may be a myriad of tongues spoken in the eternal
world; but only a human word can reach man in this
present life. To treat the word as human is essential.
We might argue that it is impossible that the eternal
God should use words at all; words are not the only
means of communication. But words that are at once
communications meant for man, and also in no language known to man, are impossible to conceive.

If words are human, they are subject to the conditions in which human beings use words. They cannot be kept out of the province of grammarian or
historian or student of literature. Words so exempted
would no longer be of any value as a means of communication to us.

But, being human, they do not cease to act as a way

of approach from God to the mind of man. If they are human, it does not mean that they can be understood without any reference to God. We cannot say that we know all about this human book and need no recourse to God. If the words can be explained without the belief that a divine voice is speaking through them, then we must accept the fact, and with it the loss of all that made life glorious. But why must we say that we understand all that a word means because it is human? Why so hastily assume that words can be explained without mystery? It is not as though we could contrast self-explanatory unmysterious words such as we use with the mysterious message of the eternal Lord. We are in reality handling something mysterious whenever we deal with words. All words are mysterious. There are no " mere words."

When therefore we enter upon the reading of the Holy Scriptures, because we know that they are in human form we must not shut our minds to the possibility that God may be waiting to meet us there. We need not choose between reading the Bible as we read other books, and some other way; we may read it as we do other books and, as Bishop Westcott confessed, we may find in it what is not to be found in any other book.

There was a noble passage in an address given by Peter T. Forsyth, a profound thinker of our times:

> Or I read the story of the father who beseeches Christ to heal his son. I hear the answer of the Lord, " I will come down and heal him." " Him! " That means me. The words are life to my distempered soul. I care little for them (when

I need them most) as a historic incident of the long past, an element in the discussion of miracles. They do not serve their divinest purpose till they come to me as they come to that father. They come with a promise here and now. I see the heavens open, and the Redeemer at the right hand of God. I hear a great voice from heaven, and these words are the words of the Saviour himself to me, " I will come down and heal him." And upon these he rises from his eternal throne, he takes his way through a ready line of angels, archangels, the high heavenly host and the glorious fellowship of the saints. They part at his coming, for they know where he would go. These congenial souls do not keep him, and these native scenes do not detain him. But on the wings of that word he moves from the midst of complete obedience, spiritual love, holy intelligence, ceaseless worship and perfect praise. He is restless in the midst of all that in search of me — me sick, falling, lost, despicable, desperate —. He comes, he finds, he heals me on the wings of those words.

When in this way our Lord comes to us in his Word, we have not ceased to read the book as it comes in human speech, but we have found in it what it was meant to give.

He seeks us in the holy communion.

God seeks us in that sacrament to which many names are given. It is the holy communion, the eucharist, the Lord's Supper, the breaking of bread. Nothing is gained by disguising the differences of belief which such words describe. Yet, since this book is not meant to be more than a piece of first aid, it is right to show wherein all Christian people agree when they take this sacrament.

All agree that whatever may be the fitting approach to worship at other times, in this hour it is one of waiting and receptivity. At other times the worshiper may be called to struggle, to fight, to wrestle; here he must expose his whole spirit to the presence and power of Another who is drawing near. He seeks, for he must always seek; but the master thought of his mind now is that he is being sought, and all that he has to do is to remove what may hinder the coming of his Lord. He enters into this scene desirous only that he may not miss the quickening and life-giving experience which is offered to him.

The given-ness of the Christian religion; the grace of it; the priority of Christ — these truths, never to be forgotten, are here set forth. The Catholics, and the Brethren who break bread on the first day of the week, are poles apart in many of their beliefs, as they are in their methods of worship. But they agree that they do not win anything for themselves, nor do they provide for themselves the substance of the feast. They have nothing which they have not received. They use the same words: " Take, eat; this is my body which is given for you." There is no escape from the truth that in the eucharist or at the Lord's table, wherever men keep the Lord's death and feed upon him by faith, they are not seekers first of all, but the sought. They do not find, they are found.

There is always the earthward side of an act of communion. It may be a poor and mean exterior to which the worshiper comes. The bread has been grown in the earth and ground in the mill. The words spoken are not magical with a power to evoke mysterious and hidden forces. The origin of the rite, whatever form it may take, can be told by students of history. Why bring in God?

No answer can be complete except in experience. The seeker after God must be ready to make experiments upon the evidence of others. Here is a rite which obviously has a human side. Why is it that the thing which is obvious to us has not been obvious to others no less able to see clearly, no less honest than we are? It should be at least conceivable that the case is not so complete as we think when we rob such a feast or celebration of its mystery. We may be perfectly right in our explanation of the earthly setting, and at the same time we may be missing something which shines through that and is found in it. It may be a very mean thing, and at the same time the upper room into which the Lord comes to eat the passover with us. That upper room in Jerusalem was like other rooms; the materials for the feast were like others provided that night; the disciples were a small company of Galileans who had come to Jerusalem with their Master. Yet when we think of that upper room we see a glory which shines upon it from an unseen world. Into that room there enters One who transfigures it, and he brings his gifts with him.

Imagine that this may be true still. That sacrament which is celebrated may have its inner side, from which a glory may break through to illuminate all things. It is at least a possibility which ought not to be dis-

missed.   Certainly over against it we have no right
to set the poverty of its outward scene, its lowly and
even shabby surroundings. We must face the claim
that the sacrament may be the means whereby the
imprisoned glory of the Lord may break upon the soul.
   In his great eucharist hymn St. Thomas wrote:

> " Therefore we, before Him bending,
>   This great sacrament revere;
>   Types and shadows have their ending
>   For the newer rite is here:
>   Faith, our outward sense befriending,
>   Makes the inward vision clear."

   Charles Wesley wrote:

> " Jesu, we thus obey
>   Thy last and kindest word,
>   Here in thine own appointed way
>   We come to meet our Lord."

Both agree that in this feast the soul comes to meet
with the unseen Lord, and through the outward sense
to have the inward vision made clear. Here the witnesses agree.
   They agree no less in their belief that it is the
Redeemer, who died and rose again, who comes to
meet the soul of man. Some serious thinkers may be
content to treat Jesus as a teacher whose words are
worthy of being repeated to all the successive generations of men. They call together their fellows to
read these words for their wisdom and beauty and
grace. They lay no stress on the fact that he who
spoke these words died on the cross. What he did

in act appears to them to belong to the past; the words only remain. But it is altogether impossible to believe in the sacrament unless in it the Saviour who redeemed men with his precious blood draws near, mighty still to save and to hold the soul.

As a matter of history this sacrament has never been separated from the thought of Christianity, as a religion not of enlightenment only, but of redemption. He who offers himself in such a fashion cannot be a teacher whose words only are to be revered. Why should men eat bread and drink wine to commemorate the words of a teacher? If this were the meaning of these signs they would be singularly unfitting, and even misleading.

Whatever varied meanings we may read into the words which we hear, "This is my body, . . . this is my blood," to every serious thinker they must have something to do with the Redeemer who has done an act of divine and eternal significance and done it for them, for me. In a sacrament there is of necessity an act remembered and prolonged.

The people of Christ agree, wherever they keep the feast, that it is the Lord as the dying Redeemer for whom they look. It is he who seeks the soul in that hour.

Seeks! This is no dead hero whose deeds we keep alive. Whatever else a sacrament means, it cannot mean merely that. On the level of our present life we children of time and space go forth to meet One who still can do for the soul all that he has ever done. His dying was at one moment in history, yet it revealed and made effective on this earthly scene in every age till the end the eternal love of God. The soul waits to meet One who in his cross commends his own changeless and inexhaustible love to us.

What does he offer? It may be put in many ways. But all the figures and images, all the types and symbols, mean this: The Redeemer giving to men thinking, willing, loving, his own life, so that they can say, " I live, and yet not I but Christ liveth in me." His life, which has passed through death, is given to the waiting soul in its hunger. This is meant to show that it is no legal acquittal which is offered to us, but a new birth and a new life. Men have been tempted to read into the Christian religion the figures of law, or of commerce, or of earthly tyrannies. But always this sacrament has been a protest against such limitation. It compels us to think of life and the nourishment of life. " Feed on him by faith in your hearts. Drink, . . . this is the blood of the new covenant." So he seeks for us here in this sacred meeting place.

He seeks, but he is the Lord of a people who comes to us. He does not come as One who can be known and received apart from his body, the church. This sacrament is always a protest against an individual piety which shrinks from its part in the fellowship. It is an act of social worship, not the lonely ecstasy of the soul. There are hours in which the soul may be alone with the Redeemer, as Mary was with Jesus in the garden on the first Easter day. " Rabboni! " we may still cry with that personal bond for our own. But he does not come thus to seek for us in the sacrament; there he is one with his people; when he died they died with him; that body, the church, was there at Calvary, and is there forever with him.

He is in that way. We must go forth to meet him
there.

In the way of surrender and obedience.

" The chapter is long," a friend remarked, " but it
cannot end without some account of another way in
which he may find us. I want somewhere in the book
to read the words of our Lord: ' He that hath my
commandments and keepeth them, he it is that loveth
me: and he that loveth me shall be loved of my Father,
and I will love him and will manifest myself to him.'
Is not that a way in which we may expect to find him?
He will manifest himself."

" That is true," I answered, " and though it may
be implied everywhere, it must be said definitely and
underlined; and long as the chapter is, it must not
end without this promise to the seeker."

There may come an hour in which we are deeply
impressed by the call of the Saviour to the life which
we see so perfectly in him. We recognize his as the
noblest life. But as yet we cannot say that we know
him as St. Paul came to know him, or St. Francis.
Are we to wait then till he has manifested himself
to us, and then go out to keep his commandments
and serve him in our love to one another? That
does not seem to be the right order, if we listen to
his words. He would rather tell us to make experiments if we would come across his path. " Faith
begins as an experiment, and ends as an experience."
He would bid us surrender ourselves to him, rise up
and follow him, and so set out upon the way along
which he will meet with us and manifest himself to us.

We should remember other words of the Saviour

spoken in the same hour: "If a man serve me, let him follow me, and where I am there shall also my servant be." Some serve without following; but the true way is to follow. And what happens to the follower? He discovers himself in new and unexpected ways in the presence of his Lord, *where he is.*

In surrender to that which calls to us and claims us, and in treading the way of obedience, we may find him or be found by him.

The words of Dr. Schweitzer, so wonderfully verified in his experience, will be verified also in ours:

> Jesus came to us as One unknown, without a name, as of old by the lakeside he came to those who knew him not; he speaks to us the same words, "Follow me," and sets us the tasks which he has to fulfill for our time. He commands. And to those who obey him, whether they be wise or simple, he will reveal himself in the toils, the conflicts, the sufferings which they shall pass through in his fellowship, and as an ineffable mystery they shall learn in their own experience who he is.

It is a simple counsel to give. We may grow impatient with it, and ask for some more distant road to take and some more difficult task to do. But here the way lies at our very door, and we may take it without waiting. It is the way of loving obedience. There he will meet us and manifest himself to us, as he has promised.

X

THE JUDGE WHO COMES TO MEET US

> His love will seek in thee till death
> A Bethlehem and Nazareth;
> He climbs the hills of Galilee
> And marches to the cross in thee;
> Thou art the garden where he lies,
> In thee the third day he will rise;
> Rejoice, great soul, when morn shall break,
> And leave thee sleeping, he will wake.

THAT God comes into our life in Christ, seeking us, is a truth at the heart of the Christian religion. The good news which was believed and preached from the beginning was this very thing — God had come, and anywhere and at any time those who looked for him might see him.

But he could only be seen in his own character and purpose. That could not be changed to meet the demands of the seeker. He might have had another character and visited men for another purpose. The same word, " God," has been used in many senses. But he *did* come to redeem his people, and they who would look with him might find him, but only as their Redeemer.

If he had been a mathematician those who would follow his way would have certain conditions to fulfill; they would need at least to be austere and disinterested lovers of truth.

If he could only be likened to an artist, such as sought him would need at least an eye quick to answer to beauty.

The God who seeks us in Christ is the God of truth and beauty, and in the search for him every noble instinct of the spirit of man has its function; but he is first of all holy Love, and the seeker must be ready for an encounter with such a Being. It must make a difference if we have to do with such a One. When therefore the good news was carried abroad that God had visited his people, there went with it the word that those who wanted to find him must remember what kind of God he was. They were on the track not of some God, but of *this* God.

He might come; he might be near at hand; he might be speaking; but whether the children of men saw him or not depended upon their own readiness for him. He had answered their needs, but they must be conscious what their needs were if the answer was to reach them; to others his words and his acts would be unknown.

Not first of all to man saying, " Give me truth " ; not to man saying, " Give me beauty," did he come, but to man saying, " Give me goodness, give me love." If that was so, the search for him must be the search of a moral being. Not to man as an intellectual explorer, not to man as an artistic creator, but to man who had come to know where he had failed and grieved his God had the Lord of the World come.

This search of man has one condition. Before a man can find his Lord he must be prepared to meet him in judgment. The day when the soul finds this Lord must be for it a day of judgment.

No one who is at all sensitive to the mind of his fellows in the present hour will expect anything but a cold reception of any talk of judgment. The word belongs to an ancient vocabulary which to them has no longer any place in the modern world. There are many reasons why the thoughtful mind revolts against some of the crude and terrible pictures of judgment which Christians have thrown upon the screen of the future. Man has read his own basest passions and lusts into the character of God. He has represented him as a torturer to whom the devices of the earthly torturer are by comparison merciful. But man's folly must not make us hastily dismiss the truth which his misunderstanding has caricatured. There is written on the conscience and mind of man the certainty of judgment, and we do not rid ourselves of that certainty by showing how the children of men have let their own bitterness and hatred run riot in their picture of their Lord. The judgment seat is not as the men of the past saw it. But there is and there must be a judgment seat.

If the moral life is anything but a delusion there must be judgment. Otherwise there would be a sowing and no harvest; a process which has no finish; history with no significance; drama without plot. We may dismiss judgment from our thoughts, but if we do so we must also dismiss the reality of the moral life. We lose the great tragedies of the world, but we lose also the New Testament; and not simply the Epistles, but the Gospels. St. Paul, it is true, reasoned with Felix concerning judgment; but Jesus, no less, told of the hour when the Son of Man should come in his glory and all the holy angels with him. And in the very important words in John our Lord says of his cross, " Now is the judgment of this world."

That expectation of judgment to which the spirit of man bears witness is confirmed in the gospel. Those who enter into the story of the gospel cannot meet with Christ without finding him their judge — the hour in which they stand before him will be the hour of judgment. You never read the Gospels till for you that judgment becomes a present reality.

As the eye adjusts itself to the Gospels it becomes fixed upon Christ crucified, and there it remains. Not that in the hour of the cross he took another part, that the one who had been before the ethical teacher or the sympathetic healer became now for the first time the Lord of judgment. In all the revelation of his life he judged men: the first response to the good news was repentance. But all the earlier scenes in the story are gathered up in this one last act in which our Lord gave himself to men. Having loved his own which were in the world, he loved them unto the end. In that end all that he had been could be read in letters of fire. But though the hour of the cross was in a distinctive sense the hour of judgment, when men remembered Jesus they remembered always that to enter into his presence at any time was to come into an experience of that very judgment of the cross. Of judgment they had heard from the prophets, and there had been a foretaste of that very hour in their own hearts. It was in one sense a new experience to meet with Jesus; in another sense they had been prepared for it all their lives.

To understand what judgment means here we do well to dismiss from our minds the analogy of the magistrates' court, or the Old Bailey. There an offender is brought to book by the quotation of laws which he has broken. He is made to see his offense by measuring his conduct against the standard laid down by the laws of the society in which he lives. It may be that he is guilty merely of breaking some necessary regulation, but not any serious expression of the moral law. Or it may be that he is condemned for some act which is at once an offense against human society and against the Christian law. But he may not discover his inward guilt in the court at all. He meets judgment, but not judgment as we meet it in Christ.

When Simon Peter came into the presence of his Lord, or when Mary anointed his feet with the precious ointment, they were judged, but not by any code or book of laws. Simon went out and wept bitterly because of something which he had seen in the eyes of Jesus. Mary anointed his feet because she had been forgiven much, and that forgiveness had been judgment for her.

We shall come nearer to the understanding of this judgment if we think in the language of personal relationship. We must think of judgment in terms of human relationship.

How, for example, is a musician to be judged? Auer was a great teacher of music in Leipzig. To that city came students of the violin from every land; they were already accomplished players, but they went to him as to a master in the highest reaches of their art. If we imagined one of them in the full tide of his career returning to the old master in after years, and playing to him, we can see what a day of judgment may mean.   The player, famous it might be in the world's eye, would listen for the judgment of his teacher. There would be no need of words of condemnation. The player would read in the face of the old master where he had been faulty and where he had fallen from his old standards.   ·

In all human relationships there is an element of judgment.   Where two human beings meet there must be an element of contrast as well as of affinity. The friend learns to know himself through the eyes of his friend; he becomes his other self.   It is one of the most fatal errors to confuse the words " individual " and "personal."   A person in reality becomes himself only in fellowship, in escaping from the individual life.   "Personality is a capacity for communion." In every relation between persons there is always something that brings them together and always something that separates them.   We discover what is lacking or wrong in ourselves when we see ourselves in contrast with another.*

That is how conviction of sin may come.   We used to hear more than we do today of these words.   It was considered the first stage toward a new life that a soul must be made aware of sin and the " exceeding sinfulness of sin."   But the awareness must often have come by way of what has been called " a conviction of righteousness "; a man knew himself to be a sinner not because he measured himself against a book of instructions and regulations, but because he saw the other kind of life in some person whom he observed and admired.   It is not any abstract con-

* This idea has been admirably expounded in H. H. Farmer, *God and the World*.

ception of virtue that will awaken us; it is goodness and love as we see them expressed in some life. Indeed there is no goodness or love except as they are incarnate. And if we are to be brought into judgment by the appeal of holiness, it will be through some person in whom the thing which we have missed or lost or betrayed is represented in flesh and blood.

When we bear these things in mind we understand a little how it was that men in the presence of Jesus were judged. They saw him, and the sight made them see themselves. They knew their sin when they saw his goodness. They were unloving, he loved with a perfect love; they were self-centered, he lived a life centered in God; they were grudging in their devotion, he held nothing back; to them God was something, to him God was everything.

More than codes or laws was needed to bring men to knowledge of themselves. More is needed still if we are to be brought to judgment. We do not think it surprising when we read that this same Lord went steadfastly to Jerusalem where as in a citadel his enemies waited for him. He must needs go, and go to judge the world. He exposed himself to them with no armor against their weapons. In the city he met with evil, but not such evil as could be discovered only once, never before and never after. The evil which was at work in Jerusalem was the evil which is always at work in human society. It is common to man; it is not strange to him. Our Lord had to deal with it in its full power.

What was new and strange was the occasion for the revelation of that evil. That occasion was the coming of the Son of God in all his holiness. Not by discourse upon virtue was the revelation made; through his own action in that hour the disguise was torn from evil. He — not his words only, but he himself in his action — made men see what it was that they lacked. Now was the judgment of the world.

Judgment must mean revelation which strips evil of its disguises. The revelation which Jesus in his life had begun to make wherever he met with men and women was perfected in the hours upon the cross. There the evil principle of the world was shown in action. *This, this* was what the sin of man meant and had meant all through the ages.

Two things are revealed in that moment: love and sin. They could only be revealed together. It was not as though an example had to be taken of man at his worst. There was nothing in that Syrian city that day which could not have been found in any city in any age. Indeed, if a comparison is to be made with other cities, Jerusalem perhaps might appear comparatively virtuous. Of the abiding gifts made by that ancient world to all time two stand out above all others: the religion of Israel and the law of Rome. Both were represented in Jerusalem. The agents by whom the crucifixion was planned were the men to whom these solemn trusts were committed; Caiaphas was the high priest of the temple, Pilate was the trustee of Roman law. And we cannot forget that Judas Iscariot, who betrayed Jesus, was one of those who had been in his circle, who had gone out to preach the coming of the kingdom and to heal the sick in his name. Here were safeguards. The world had none better to offer. Why did they fail?

In such a scene the coming of the holy Son of God meant the hour of revelation; not of something wrong in law, or even in religion, but in human beings. Something had entered into human society which could never be attacked unless it was first laid bare. It could never be laid bare except as its power could be measured in its action upon a person; and only the most holy One could be the occasion for the unmasking of that evil. There were many philosophers in that day who could have analyzed the evil in human society, who could have exposed Pontius Pilate and Caiaphas and Judas. To this day scholars are ready to study in the school of Seneca, who was a contemporary of Paul. Seneca would have seen through the motives of the actors of that day. The actors themselves understood one another. Caiaphas played upon the weakness of Pilate who was held by the dead hand of his own past; Pilate saw that " for envy " the priests had given up Jesus to him. There was no lack of intellectual judgment.

But if men were to know themselves without any disguises more was needed than the analysis made by wise men. They must see the meaning of their actions not as the actions concerned their own individual lives, but as they were part of a great pattern. They must discover what they meant to the mind of the Lord of the World, who has a purpose for all mankind. What did men themselves do to him when he put himself in their power? If they could see the meaning of that action, written not in words but in deeds, not through someone who can understand the human standpoint only, but through someone who can

see things from the side of God, they might know a
little what sin means. Not crime, nor folly, but *sin.*
They might cry once more, " Against thee, thee only
have I sinned."

This recognition took place, and still takes place,
when men are drawn to the cross. They come to that
historic cross knowing that it symbolizes a miscarriage
of justice, but they remain there with other thoughts.
They see what the cross revealed of the principle of
evil in the agents who sent Jesus to it. He was " crucified under Pontius Pilate ": all that this involved they
begin to measure; but they know that there is more to
be learned than an account of certain acts done in
an eastern city long ago. To stand before the cross
of Christ is a more personal experience than that; it
is a day of judgment, not for Pilate, not for Caiaphas,
but for you and me.

You can find God in the cross; but he must be first
of all the God who judges and reveals. It is in Christ
crucified that the soul discovers the utmost limit of
its own sin. The self-centeredness of the life which we
are living cannot be easily perceived in the swift stream
of events. If we are to be judged we must be helped
to see the sin, so easily disguised, in the full measure
of its power. Egoism seems a trifling charge for us
to bring against ourselves; to understand its evils we
must see it carried out to its last measure. What if
that living for myself, that self-centeredness, is the
sin which is at the root of the white slave traffic,
sweated labor, the oppression of child races, war? To
know my sin I must see it magnified on that vast
scale; but even so I may not have entered deeply into
the last realities. How can I see my life in its relation

to the eternal and holy God? Only, once more, as I am ready to face the contrast with myself, the perfection embodied in the holy Son of God. That is one of the experiences to which the soul is exposed before the cross.

The God and Father of our Lord Jesus Christ is a holy God, in whose light we must seek to come to an understanding of ourselves as he must see us. It is not with ourselves as creatures of time, in contrast with his eternal life, that we are concerned, nor with ourselves as limited beings in the presence of the Infinite. God differs from us in that he is loving and we fail in love, he forgives and we are unforgiving. When he speaks to us his last word, it is in the life of One who, in his love, died for his own and for their sakes suffered all that needed to be borne to set them free.

All that this sacrifice means we cannot know. Nor is it necessary to wait till we comprehend clearly how on his cross the Saviour bore our sins and carried our sorrows. There is truth in the lines of the hymn:

> " But none of the ransomed ever knew
> How deep were the waters crossed."

We do not know, and cannot know, the death that he died. It is enough for us at the beginning of our new life that the light falls upon us, the searching light from the face of the Crucified.

Judgment means revelation; but more than that: it means also destruction. God kills and makes alive. The judgment is not to be separated from the mercy of God. Judgment is mercy, even as wrath is the recoil of love from evil. The soul which is exposed to the revelation of evil has within it the secret of the destruction of evil. The One who meets us in the gospel is rich in mercy; if he were not, he would never let us know the terror of his love. " The soul is consumed and quickened" by him; consumed, or it could never be quickened; quickened by the love which will not spare it.

But they who yielded to him passed out of that day of judgment into the riches of his love. One who knew what that experience meant said, " There is therefore now no condemnation for them that are in Christ Jesus." For him the judgment was over, and in all his experience, bitter as it had been, it was the same Lord who drew near to him.

Judge because he was Saviour, Saviour because he was Judge.

Like a solemn refrain of great music, the thought of his coming to us is repeated in the Scriptures; and he is always the same:

" The Son of Man is come to seek and to save that which was lost."

" Ye have not chosen me but I have chosen you."

" The Son is come to give his life a ransom for many."

" This is love, not that we loved God but that he loved us."

" He loved me and gave himself for me."

" Behold I stand at the door and knock."

This is the wonder of the gospel. But it must not be halved by us. We cannot read it as an offer of a reformation in human society or as tidings of a general amnesty. Rather is it first of all revelation, judgment, destruction. The answer to it is repentance, the ad-

justment of life to a new Lord. With this revelation
there will come to the soul that will accept it deliverance, forgiveness, peace.

You can find God: but only such a God can be
found.

XI

CAN SEEKERS FIND NOW?

Because the hinds have sought the brooks
   Through ages past, the panting hind
Today for living water looks;
   They found, and she will find.

Because the saints have sought, I seek
   For God in wildernesses dry,
And since they found I, lost and weak,
   Shall find him ere I die.

WE MUST seek, we shall find; but shall we find —
now? Or is it characteristic of this life in time that
we must spend it in seeking, and of the life beyond
death that then for the first time we may find? This
question has still to be answered. It is not a new
question; it has been put and answered in various ways.

The thinkers of the Middle Ages tried to reason
out the character of the blessed life in paradise. They
said that it was a life of attainment and peace. They
used the word "fruition." In paradise the redeemed
were at peace in the will of God. They were not
striving for a higher place in some other circle of the
heavenly company. They were no longer on pilgrimage. The things that they had desired and striven to
gain they now had. Their chief end was always to
glorify God, now that they enjoyed him forever.

There are moderns who do not reject this doctrine, but who find it unwelcome and almost unintelligible. They conceive of life always in terms of movement from good to better, on and always on; life for them is good for this very reason, that in it man seeks. And how can any life in which the struggle is over be attractive to them? They make a concession to tradition when they sing their hymns. They say of Jerusalem the golden:

> "There is the throne of David,
> And there, from care released,
> The song of them that triumph,
> The shout of them that feast — "

but such a Jerusalem does not attract them as it did their fathers. They share the longing of the American general who hoped for a brief rest after death and then a new cry, " Fall in for Jupiter! " and once more he would arise and join the fighting men.

Without doubt this was the accepted creed in the days, not long ago, when progress was not something men doubted or denied, but a dogma beyond all question. What was more natural than to picture the life of the spirit as a perpetual progress, to conceive of the soul as always seeking, never satisfied? Even when the eye sought to catch the outlines of the other life, it saw still a life of work in progress.*

Men fell into the serious error of thinking of the life beyond death as a continuance of this life. Eternity became only an infinitely long time; and since they could not think of life on earth except in terms

* Upon this subject there is an invaluable lecture by Philip Wicksteed, *The Religion of Time and of Eternity.*

of movement, they could not picture its sequel as anything but the same, only prolonged. Much has come to shake that dogma of progress, and many have begun to inquire whether it is enough to think of life as a seeking only; whether there is not in the vision of eternity a place for fruition, and whether it is not given to man even here in time and within the limitations of time to find, as well as to seek.

It is indeed doubtful whether the heart of man was ever satisfied with the idea that life was worthless except as a scene of progress. Youth, in some leisurely discussion of such matters from a comfortable armchair, may declare that the ideal life is one of ceaseless activity, but the charwoman is likely to think of it as a rest from toil.

A religious life which is all seeking is not complete. It may become, at the worst, the life of one who is always sending his shoes to be repaired and never wears them. Perpetual " progress " may be little less than perpetual failure.

The language of those who have a right to be heard on this matter is clear. Great Christians have told us of their desperate struggles and the agony of their seeking, but they have also told us how they entered into the joy of their Lord even here, and beyond death they looked to find all that joy crowned in the peace of God:

> " I hope to see these things again,
>   But not as once in dreams of night."

We may take their witness almost at random. St. Paul, at the end, looked for the crown of glory which his Lord had laid up for him, but even in this life he knew seasons of peace and had a foretaste of the blessed kingdom of God, whether in the body or out of the body he knew not. St. Augustine and his mother, Monica, knew one evening at Ostia what it meant to pass out of the tumults of time into the joy of the Lord. Bunyan beheld such a vision in the land of Beulah, and by faith followed his pilgrims into the city of God and heard the music and wished himself among them. Oliver Cromwell wrote once to his daughter Bridget telling her that there was only one company happier than the seekers, and that was the finders. It has indeed been the witness of the people of God that they *did* find even in this life. Not everything, but something; not the thing itself in all its glory, but an earnest of it.

No hint is given us in the New Testament of the way in which the two experiences are to be reconciled. If a reader declares impatiently, " I cannot see how I can be both seeking and finding," and demands a logical account of the life in which these two experiences are known together, he will ask in vain. Our Lord and his apostles do not hesitate to tell men that they must seek and go on seeking to the end, and yet that they can find even before they leave this earthly life. " My joy I give unto you," the Lord has said; " not as the world giveth give I unto you. . . . Peace I leave with you."

In one of the greatest of all religious poems Christopher Smart wrote of the Christian inheritance:

> " Where ask is have, where seek is find,
>   Where knock is open wide."

That is a true picture of the realm into which our Lord invites his disciples. They will most certainly find.

When we consider the words of our Lord, we are amazed to discover how much is promised in them. We read, for example, the Beatitudes. We dwell much upon the life to which they call men — that wild, strange, topsy-turvy life in which all the accepted values of human society are reversed. We are startled by the thought that this sermon was probably given to those who were about to be baptized in the early church. If they asked, " What kind of life shall we be called to live? " their teachers would say, " Listen to these words." Men are instructed to be poor in spirit, meek, pure in heart, mourners, hungry and thirsty after righteousness. They are challenged to live a life which is not merely a variation of the common life; they are to strike out on fresh ways, and they must not shrink from paying the price.

As we read these words, we see those who accept them as a body of sufferers deprived of all that makes this human scene a place of happiness and wealth. We see them poor, outcast, exiled from the great human inheritance. All this they endure for their Lord's sake. They are seeking another country and for the present they must do without what others possess. We see them in the light of the things which they forfeit for the sake of their Lord.

But are we doing justice to the plain meaning of the words of our Lord? He called these men " happy "; he gave to them not only a call, but a perfectly definite promise. It may be worth while to put these promises down in their order:

Blessed are the poor in spirit: *for theirs is the kingdom of heaven.*

Blessed are they that mourn: *for they shall be comforted.*

Blessed are the meek: *for they shall inherit the earth.*

Blessed are they which do hunger and thirst after righteousness: *for they shall be filled.*

Blessed are the merciful: *for they shall obtain mercy.*

Blessed are they which are persecuted for righteousness' sake: *for theirs is the kingdom of heaven.*

Blessed are ye when men shall revile you and persecute you and say all manner of evil against you falsely, for my sake. *Rejoice and be exceeding glad: for great is your reward in heaven: for so persecuted they the prophets which were before you.*

This is a picture of these disciples not in some other sphere of life, but here in this realm of time and space. We see a number of men and women who have great treasures, wealth to be enjoyed beyond all the dreams of misers. Theirs is the realm of heaven: they are comforted; they inherit the earth; they hunger no more; they obtain mercy; they enter into the company of the prophets and rejoice and are exceeding glad; they leap for joy. Clearly such disciples are not encouraged to look upon this life simply as a scene of conflict and loss; it is not in negatives that such a life can be fully described. The negative is clearly set down: there are ways which they may not tread;

there are treasures which they cannot possess. But there is a gloriously positive future before them; and when they are called happy it is not simply in respect of their losses, but also because of the rich gains which they can have. As seekers they are happy, but they are happy also as finders.

In their education for life a place of first importance is given to prayer. But prayer as our Lord interpreted it is not asking only, or seeking, or knocking. It is a real cooperation with God: real, not make-believe! The disciple is called to ask, and he shall receive; to knock, and the door shall be opened to him; to seek, and he shall find.

In one of his many promises the Master said: " Be of good cheer; in the world ye shall have tribulation, but be of good cheer, I have overcome the world." Here there is the same attempt to put side by side the two apparently contradictory experiences — tribulation, and triumph; pressed down by the world, liberated by the victorious Lord; bond, and free; dying, and behold they will live. The disciples have not to choose between two experiences. It is not as though some disciples were to endure affliction and others sing the song of victory; or as though in one mood a disciple would be cast down, and in another exalted. The much more difficult undertaking entered into by the Lord for his people is to make them both at the same time — hard-pressed, and free; in the grip of the world, and yet able to defy the world. The enemy will stand over them, and then, as Bunyan said, will come " the sound of the silver trumpet and the trampling of the slain! "

To the tempted soul also there is promised the

same twofold life. Men will not know until the end cessation of conflict. There will never come a time when the soul will not need to watch. After his own temptations in the wilderness the Lord had peace, but only for a time. The tempter departed from him for a season. He himself left with his friends the counsel that they must watch and pray. St. Paul has left to all men the picture of human life as a battlefield in which the enemies are not flesh and blood, a field on which there is never a call to stand at ease. Having overcome, stand — ready for the next attack!

Yet to the same souls, set in the midst of foes, there is promised a taste of victory even here. Sins are forgiven them. It is not in the future alone that they will enter into the restored relationship of children to their Father. They can know and confirm the truth of the words spoken by their Lord many times, "Thy sins are forgiven thee." And forgiveness means this at least: the old bond is re-formed; the prodigal is home again. Once more, if this contradiction cannot be easily solved in logic, it has been solved in Christian experience.

Where do we go for an account of the nature and horror of sin? Not to those who are held by the chains of evil habit. There comes a time when that which should make them aware of their condition ceases to act. As St. Paul put it, "They are past feeling." It is to the saints who overcome that we turn for an account of sin. Because they are out of its power they can see it, and not only that; because they are resisting it they can measure its power. Who can tell the terrors of a journey through a strange country but the man who has made it, and made it to the end?

At the same time these authorities upon sin speak with quiet certainty of the peace given them by their Lord. They are still seeking victory but at the same time they are enjoying victory.

" But what is God to those who find? " one may ask. The Lord is kind to those who seek; but what is he to those who find? There is no answer to that question save that what is found passes the power of tongue or pen to show. It is the secret which cannot be passed on by any word of man. The experience is one to which there can be no perfect analogy. We cannot say of it, " It is like this and that."

> " The love of Jesus, what it is
> None but his loved ones know."

Yet there are certain things which can be said of the finders; or rather, certain things can be said of that experience of the soul when it is no longer seeking, but rejoicing in the gift of God which it has found.

The seeker reads the Word, and the seeker who has found also reads it. It is the same collection of books that is available to both, and the books all have the same meaning to the student of the text. The historical records do not change whatever the spiritual disposition of the reader may be. But there *is* a difference for the soul which has found or, as St. Paul said, been found.

If we have found him of whom these writers speak, then we pass through the words to that which lies behind and within the words. On the wings of the words there comes to us the assurance that the living God is speaking to us. We speak of this assurance in the language of personal relationships: he is Father, Lord, Friend; but such words, the best that we know, are only pointers. They show at least that this approach to the soul is not less than personal. All that "personal" can convey is found in this word and action of God. *How much more* will God himself be to us Father, Lord, Friend!

It is not alone of Isaiah or Jeremiah or the apostles that we are thinking. In their experience we find ourselves. The God who spoke to them and laid his hand upon them in the same records speaks to us. There is a new meaning for us in the old word. There is the witness of the Spirit. Through the Spirit there is given a message old but new to us. No new word, but one which we have had from the beginning; but it comes fresh to us, as though we were the first to hear the word of the Good Shepherd or to feel the pressure of that Lord who besets man behind and before. To have found is to enter into the scene, not as readers, but as living souls, exposed to the burning and shining light of God who draws near to us, to me.

What is he to those who find him in his church? The church is a place for seekers. But when they find they have a new experience. Every part of the service is charged with a new meaning. The service becomes an experience for which the word "personal" is not enough, and yet it must be used. In the church the soul is one of a company which no man can number. Its voice is raised in the song which only the redeemed can sing. Ten thousand others are with the solitary soul. They are making their answer to One who has sought them and found them. They are not simply seeking something more for themselves; they are rejoicing in the gift of God to them.

There are many reasons why I should go to church. Among them this should never be forgotten: I should go to take my part in the song of a redeemed world in answer to its Redeemer. A seeker I must always be, but if I have met in the ways of life with this Redeemer, and been found by him, I must go to rejoice with all those who share this experience of the glorious love of God, which is now mine in part, and will be mine wholly forever.

WHAT IF YOU DO FIND?

THERE are moments in which, as life nears its close, we go back in memory to its early days. One picture from the past comes back to the writer of this book. It will serve to bring my word to its end. It is the picture of a Lancashire Sunday school of which I was a member. I can still call to mind those who were boys there when I was a boy. Many of them were weavers who would be called early on Monday mornings to go to their looms. The Sunday school had, and still has, a place of honor in the life of Lancashire, and anyone who has belonged to it will always remember it with gratitude. We met in the school before we went to our classes, and we sang hymns the refrains of which still come back to me. It cannot be claimed that they were always good hymns or that the music was beautiful. Many of them were deposits from the revivals of the past. But truths were preserved in them which shine more brightly after many years. One chorus ran:

> " There is life for a look at the Crucified One,
> There is life at this moment for thee."

There have been times in which such jingles have seemed poor and unworthy. The lines themselves may be taken to mean little more than a crude and almost superstitious belief. But the years have made it seem less important to discover where such a call may be abused than to hold fast to the truth which breaks through the words.

There *is* life for a look at the Crucified One! The one purpose of this book has been to clear the way for that critical moment in which we can look at him and, looking, begin to live.

A look! Can it change all things? It was true of Job: " I had heard of thee with the hearing of the ear, but now mine eye seeth thee." It was true of Isaiah: " In the year that King Uzziah died, I saw the Lord high and lifted up " ; that look meant new life for the young noble of Jerusalem. It was true of Simon Peter, who began a new life when " the Lord turned and looked upon him and he went out and wept bitterly." It was true of Saul of Tarsus when a light brighter than the sun blinded him and he heard the voice of the Crucified: " I am Jesus, and thou art persecuting me." It was true of St. Augustine, St. Francis of Assisi, Ramon Lull, St. Francis Xavier. They looked and lived. They might have turned away and been lost to the service of God in this world. Others might have taken their crown. Others, indeed, had that strange sight offered to them, glanced at it and passed on; but these looked to the Crucified and their destiny was sealed at once and for all time. They looked and lived.

There come hours in life in which the accumulated experiences of years are fused into one act and there is set before us a choice between this way and that. Such a choice becomes an epitome of all the choices of all our days. It becomes in the end a question of

which way we are to look. On the one hand there are
voices which call us to a life of adventure and hazard,
the only reward of which must be sought in the love
of Christ; on the other hand every fiber of our being
is made to feel the pull of the world of sensible things
— the comfort, the pride, the glory of it all. We may
deliberately look this way or that.

In the story of the cities of the plain we read that
Lot's wife looked back and was turned into a pillar
of salt; she looked and died! Of course we do not
look deliberately towards the cities of the plain, though
there are such cities still and it is not counted so
shameful a thing in these days as once it was to have
residence in them. But for most of those who once
were living and now are dead columns, shining in
their whiteness, the choice was not between looking
back to the cities of the plain or away to the hills.
They were not tempted by any such manifest corruption as that which filled Sodom and Gomorrah.
They looked back to a scene which offered ease and
wealth, and perhaps fame, provided that the price of
conformity to its standards was duly paid. But that
look determined the character of their days. Such
a look is not a passing glance, it is the response of the
heart to one of two alternatives which have been before it for long. It is the look of decision, the look
of the lover who has made his choice; and there is
destiny in that look.

You can look and live. You can also look and pass
out of life.

By all means let us read into the word "salvation"
as full a meaning as we can. Let us take life to be the
scene in which man, by yielding himself to Christ,

comes to his true self.   Let us include in the redeemed
life all beauty and truth and holiness.   But we need not
think that we can change the character of the spiritual
world.   It is still through the look of the soul upon the
Crucified one that the way lies to life.   " There *is* life at
this moment for thee."

But so tremendous an experience can be had only
in a world which offers hazards.   Life can be a real
adventure only on the understanding that there are
perils to be met and that something real hangs upon
the quest.   To walk along a level plain offers no risks,
but the mountaineer can win the thrill and the glory
of his days only by running risks.   And if there is
life in a look, that can be only if it is also understood
that there may be loss of life in a look.   If with all
deliberation, and in full awareness of what the issue
means, the soul looks back, then, so far as its value
as a living force in the world can be estimated, it has
ceased to be.   Only a cold and lifeless column rises
to warn other pilgrims.

But what will follow if we look?   What is this life
of which we speak?   We may think of it as the lowest
possible measure of change, or we may dare to claim
the miracles which can still be repeated.

Faith, like all things human, can be studied in its
weakness or in its strength.   In its weakness it may
be little more than a faint and trembling desire, with
little courage and little hope in it.   All that can be
claimed for it on that level is that it is not unbelief;
and in the desperate situation which faces mankind
" he that is not against us is on our part."   But why
should the man who has found God be measured
by this mean standard?   Is it the way of such a God

as the Father of our Lord Jesus Christ to offer his Spirit grudgingly?

On the contrary, there is wealth beyond measure for the surrendered soul. There are adventures to be run; there is a life of endless fascination.

You find God. In one swift glance you see him, and you know that you are his forever. But you have still your life to live on this earth. You are in a world which is God's world, and you must walk with him there. You will have all your powers to offer to him for his use. You will be a citizen of your own city and nation, you will belong to the family of God in all the world, and in all the many ways of your life you will be henceforth pledged to your Lord.

The beginning of the new life comes when you seek and, in seeking, meet the Redeemer who is seeking you. That is the beginning; but what will follow? A lifetime, if so it may be, in which all that is given in that one look will be worked out in patient service to your own age.

There is a just revolt against the belief that the individual soul can separate itself from the community. No ladder is offered you by which you can escape; rather, a place in the throng, where men are suffering and fighting a hard battle, where the Captain of our salvation calls for his own to walk the lines with him. It is not the part of the redeemed soul to evade the obligations to the common life. In that common life Christ is still to be found. The soul that has once found him in his Word and in his sacrament must still seek for him. It will be a sign that a man has really found him if he discovers him where he said he would be.

" I sought thee 'mong the leaves,
　　I found thee on the dry and blasted tree,
　I found thee not until I saw the thieves
　　There crucified with thee." *

We must still see him where men are suffering and dying. He has given us his promise to meet us in the scenes of human sorrow and pain and want. " I was hungry and ye gave me meat, sick and ye visited me." But when? " Inasmuch as ye did it unto the least of these my brethren, ye did it unto me."

The last prayer of the soul.
In an ever deepening faith, which answers to an ever unfolding love, you can find God.

" Long have I played, my Lord, the hearer's part,
　　And many words of thine are known to me;
　From Hermon and Gennesaret my heart
　　Has had thy gifts; but now I must have thee.

" In token of thy love to the world's end
　　Pour'd out, the bread and wine thou gavest me;
　Thy guest am I, and thou a lavish Friend;
　　I take the signs, but hunger still for thee.

" My gold, my hours, my hands and feet I give,
　　But since thou covetest not mine but me,
　It were not just if I were doom'd to live
　　Content with thine, when I am seeking thee.

* Dora Greenwell.

" Less for a slave, but I am not a slave;
    Less for a friend, but more than friends are we;
I — a lost part of thee, thou cam'st to save —
    I, found at last, demand not thine but thee.

" Enough; since neither thou nor I can rest,
    Heart of the world, I bring the secret key
That opens ev'ry door within my breast.
    Me thou canst have. *And now I must have thee.*"

ACKNOWLEDGMENTS

THE author wishes to express his thanks to the following authors and publishers for permission to quote extracts from their publications: To Laurence Binyon, for permission to quote from *The Sirens* (Macmillan); to Victor Gollancz, Ltd., and Edmond Fleg for a quotation from the latter's *Life of Moses*; to Sheed and Ward, for a quotation from Johannes Jørgensen's *Autobiography*; to Longmans, Green and Co., Ltd., for quotations from *The Life of Romanes*, by Ethel Romanes; to J. M. Dent and Sons, Ltd., for a quotation from Baron von Hügel's *Letters to a Niece*; to Walter de la Mare, for a quotation from *Peacock Pie* (Constable); to Faber and Faber, Ltd., for a quotation from *The Rock*, by T. S. Eliot.

Pg. 15, 123